HOW
SOCIAL
WORK
CHANGED
HAWAI'I
FROM PRACTICE
TO SOCIAL JUSTICE

HOW
SOCIAL
WORK
CHANGED
HAWAI'I
FROM PRACTICE
TO SOCIAL JUSTICE

TOM COFFMAN

WATERMARK
PUBLISHING

ISBN 978-1-948011-91-4

Library of Congress Control Number: 2022945878

Photos of John A. Burns and Jack Hall (courtesy of *The Honolulu Advertiser*) from the author; Franklin D. Roosevelt courtesy of the Franklin D. Roosevelt Presidential Library and Museum; Lyndon B. Johnson courtesy of the LBJ Presidential Library; Clorinda Low Lucas and Myron Thompson courtesy of Lita and Tia Blankenfeld; Ah Quon McElrath from the University of Hawai`i Center for Labor Studies; Masaru Oshiro courtesy of the Oshiro family; Lynette Paglinawan, Patti Lyons, Andrew Chang and Susan Chandler, courtesy of the subjects

Design and production
Ingrid Lynch

Watermark Publishing
1000 Bishop St., Ste. 806
Honolulu, HI 96813
Telephone 1-808-587-7766
Toll-free 1-866-900-BOOK
sales@bookshawaii.net
www.bookshawaii.net

10 9 8 7 6 5 4 3 2 1

Printed in Korea

Contents

**In memory of
Jeanette Emiko Matsumoto,
a voice for social justice**

Introduction

The impetus for this book arose from social workers who wanted their profession to be understood, not only in terms of compassion but an *active* passion to make a better world. They looked back to look forward. They worried that the fire of the *social justice* dimension of social work was at best smoldering, and they wanted to fan the embers.

The conversation turned to the 1960s and 1970s as years of reform and innovation. Sometimes turbulently, sometimes from deeply painful problems, new approaches to social issues arose during this time. Ideas generated in disparate communities by disparate conflicts were tested, consolidated, and elevated into new programs and new standards. The most obvious context was statehood for Hawai'i in 1959. This singular event related seamlessly to a national outpouring of social and anti-poverty legislation—the Great Society project—that representatives of Hawai'i helped to mold and the government of Hawai'i eagerly embraced. Most prominently, in 1964 this wave of social support included the Economic Opportunity Act and the Civil Rights Act, and in 1965 the passage of Medicare, Medicaid, additions to the Elementary and Secondary Education Act, a colorblind immigration system and a voting rights act.

Less obviously, on the homefront the question of social justice was arising from the revival of Native Hawaiian consciousness. The histories of the 1893 overthrow of the Native Hawaiian government and the 1898 American takeover of the Hawaiian Islands were being unearthed.

Widely varied protests made headlines, and Native Hawaiian cultural practices were being more quietly revisited. Prominently in this process of change, social work was being adapted to serve as a culturally based force of regeneration.

All of this went into our discussions of how to focus the more activist, justice-oriented dimension of social work. The original voice was that of Jeanette Emiko Matsumoto, a social worker at the Queen Lili'uokalani Children's Center and the State Department of Human Services, a president of the Hawai'i chapter of the National Association of Social Workers, and later a leader of the Hawaii Government Employees Association. Jeanette mobilized two close friends, Debbie Shimizu and Sharon Otagaki. Sharon had been assistant to the dean of the University of Hawai'i School of Social Work and also a longtime public school social worker, including twelve years on the Wai'anae Coast of O'ahu. Debbie frequently has worked at the intersection of social activism and politics, including formation of policy in the Office of the Governor and development of professional standards as executive director of the Hawai'i Chapter of the National Association of Social Work. After Jeanette's untimely passing in 2012, the idea of a book about social justice work lived on, attracting the enthusiastic participation of Christine Langworthy, who for much of her career had overseen the field practicum of advanced students at the School of Social Work; and Susan Chandler, a professor of social work and public administration, eight-year director of the State Department of Human Services, and ten-year director of the College of Social Sciences Public Policy Center.

Altogether, these four veteran professionals brought to the conversation a wealth of experience in policy-making, teaching, mentoring, and hands-on social work. To them belongs the determination and depth of experience to move this project forward.

As a field coordinator for the Community Action Program in the 1960s, I was at least slightly more than an outlier in the world of social work. I had become acquainted with dozens of social workers, most inspirationally Myron B. Thompson, whose name lives on in the Thompson School of Social Work at UH. Thereafter I was hired as a reporter for the *Honolulu Star-Bulletin* to cover the state capitol, in part because I knew something about the existence of poverty and social disorganization. Coincidentally, Myron Thompson became the administrative director of the governor of Hawai'i, John A. Burns, in a historical moment when social workers were making policy in the top reaches of state and local government.

At the time this seemed like a natural progression, but in retrospect it emerges as the historic apex of a long upward arc of socially concious work that developed norms, programs, and laws, many of which endure today.

The five of us asked ourselves where and why social workers had played pivotal roles. To what extent had the goal of social justice been nurtured within the field of social work and opened the way to reform and innovation? These were unusual questions, in that people are conditioned by an inheritance of small thoughts about social work. Mostly the workers are out of sight, assigned to the seemingly endless problems of the poor, the troubled, and the disadvantaged. Social workers are expected to staunch the bleeding and bandage the wounds. If anyone encounters a social worker, it is likely because something is not going well.

Social work, it occurred to us, typically is not understood as a profession possessing a history, let alone making history. Yet it has, and it does. And even now, as we attempt to capture some of its most salient aspects, that history continues to unfold. ✦

GREAT DEPRESSION, NEW DEAL

Franklin D.
Roosevelt

SUGAR STRIKE, DOCK STRIKE

Jack Hall
ILWU

1933·39   1946·49

**Clorinda
Low Lucas**

Hawai'i's
pioneer
social worker

**Ah Quon
McElrath**

Empowering
Hawai'i's
working class

**Myron B.
Thompson**

"Hawai'i's
ultimate
social worker"

**Masaru
Oshiro**

Social
conscience
and healer

DEMOCRATIC REVOLUTION, STATEHOOD

GREAT SOCIETY, HAWAIIAN RENAISSANCE

John A.
Burns

Lyndon B.
Johnson

1954·59 1964·68

Lynette Paglinawan

Reviving and teaching *hoʻoponopono*

Patti Lyons

Exposing and criminalizing child abuse

Andrew Chang

Administrator inspired by youth work

Susan Chandler

Activist, social worker, scholar

PART I

Searching for Ancestors

CHAPTER 1

Clorinda Low Lucas

When our discussion group thought aloud about the origins of contemporary social work in Hawai'i, agreement came readily. Clorinda Low Lucas was a Native Hawaiian social worker before social work in Hawai'i was widely recognized as a profession. To overcome this limitation, she acquired a top-flight education in New York in the mid-1930s. She then returned home in the context of the Great Depression to help implement the social safety net of the New Deal. She challenged the stinginess of welfare payments and promoted the genuine engagement of workers with clients. Perhaps most remarkably, she pivoted toward a social work based on cross-cultural understanding. Born in the late nineteenth century, her influence continues into the twenty-first century.

Clorinda Lucas's early story, uncannily defined by historic figures, is about abiding inner conflict. Her grandmother was Pamaho'a Napolean, a loyalist of the Kingdom of Hawai'i with close ties to the Hawaiian monarchy. Pamaho'a had fifteen children, the eighth of whom was Clorinda's mother, Elizabeth, or Lizzie. Clorinda was to say that Lizzie grew up in a very white, Western way, a very haole way. As a small child Lizzie attended Kawaiaha'o Church, where a young attor-

Clorinda Low Lucas (1895-1986), a consummate professional, was Hawai'i's pioneer social worker.

ney, Sanford Dole, taught her Sunday school class. Childless, Sanford Dole pleaded with Pamaho'a for permission to adopt Lizzie. According to the legend, Pamaho'a rejected Dole's request for Western adoption but agreed to a Hawaiian hānai arrangement of child-rearing. Lizzie subsequently ran away from the Doles a dozen times but eventually settled into the household of Sanford and his invalid wife.

During this late 19th-century period, the Hawaiian monarchy struggled to fend off the combined pressures of the sugar planters and the United States government. The indigenous population was in a state of mass trauma on many levels, having fallen to about 40,000 people from an original ten to twenty times that number. The family-farmed taro fields were decimated. Displaced Hawaiians, impoverished and despairing, congregated in neighborhoods around the port of Honolulu, such as Kakaʻako, Pālama and Kalihi. Separated from systems that had sustained them for centuries, Hawaiians were being described as lazy, inept, and fated to disappear. One influential Christian minister described Hawaiians as "babes in character and intellect."[1]

As Lizzie was growing up, she performed compassionate work that foreshadowed the career path of her daughter Clorinda. She helped start a Hawaiian benevolent society named Hui O ʻIwi, referring to the bones of the ancestors, which suggested an awareness of the great days of Hawaiian civilization. She was also a founding member of the Hawaiian Humane Society, which began out of concern for animals and widened its scope to deprived and abused children. Lizzie married Eben Low, a renowned Hawaiian cowboy and later rancher of Hawaiʻi Island. Meanwhile, Sanford Dole had played a leading role in the overthrow of the monarchy and was named president of the (white) Provisional Government. The year Clorinda was born, 1895, was the same year that Hawaiian royalists attempted a counter-revolt, which the Provisional Government put down by armed force.

The deposed Queen Liliʻuokalani was locked in a second-floor chamber of ʻIolani Palace. A faux Republic was declared based on voting rights for moneyed white people and any odd Hawaiian male who might swear on a Bible to renounce the queen. Hawaiian school children were forbidden to speak the Hawaiian language in class, on pain

---

1 Merry, Sally Engle, *Colonizing Hawaiʻi, The Cultural Power of Law*, (Princeton, N.J., Princeton University Press, 2000), 130. Originally a statement by a prominent minister, the Rev. Sereno E. Bishop, this phrase caught the eye of the author Lawrence Fuchs, then Merry, who organized a large group of such denigrating quotations, 128-131, e.g, "The natives have the virtue of hospitality, good nature, and honesty; but they are incorrigibly indolent and have no more care for the morrow than the American Indian."

of ridicule and corporal punishment.

Possibly Dole was conflicted by what he and his fellow American descendants had wrought. Ignoring his duties as president, he retreated in anguish to Hawai'i Island, where he sought shelter and solace with Lizzie and her husband Eben. Mrs. Dole said Sanford was suffering from brain fever. After six weeks, he returned to lobby for the annexation of Hawai'i to the United States. He became, in succession, president of the makeshift Republic of Hawai'i and then the first presidentially appointed governor of the US Territory of Hawai'i.

Accordingly, Clorinda grew up in the cultural and psychological space between Eben Low's Hawai'i Island and the heavy hand of the white oligarchy in Honolulu. After eleven years of ranch life, she was sent off to Punahou School, which had been founded by Sanford's father, Daniel Dole. On Sundays, she went to a weekly brunch at the Dole house. As a teenager, she followed the lead of her mother, volunteering for benevolent work on behalf of needy Hawaiians. On graduation from high school, she went away to the elite Smith College outside of Boston.

She recalled crying every night for four months and would describe herself as part of an entire people who had been made to feel belittled and diminished. She grappled with the demons of depression and confusion that ensued from advice such as that of her mother, who told her, "You are going to live in a haole world. You had better learn how to be [haole]."[2]

"It was hard for Hawaiians to do a lot of things," Clorinda was to recall. "We thought everybody else knows more than we do or can do things better." Her repeated narrative was about building inner strength while preparing to help others do so. She said that struggling through awful times led to her life's work: "I found new courage and self-confidence—enough to move ahead."[3]

She had planned to study for two years at Smith College but stayed

---

2 Iris B. Carlton-LaNey and Christine S. Main, "Clorinda Low Lucas: Hawai'i's Social Work Pioneer", Social Service Review, June 2010, University of Chicago, 286

3 Ibid 302

Clorinda Lucas with mother, Elizabeth Low. Their family was close to both deposed Queen Liliʻuokalani and to Sanford Dole, who led the overthrow of the Hawaiian Kingdom.

LOYALISTS OF SPAIN LAUNCH CRUCIAL DRIVE

Begin Violent Attack West of Madrid; May Be Decisive Battle of War

Fascists Claim To Have Repulsed Assaults; Basques In North On Offensive

HENDAYE, France, July 8. (AP)—What may prove one of the most decisive battle of the Spanish civil w a r w a s

Welfare Head

Mrs. Clorinda Low Lucas, kamaaina social worker, returned from the mainland today to assume her new duties as city-county director of public welfare. Mrs. Lucas

GATES OF CITY CLOSED AFTER NIGHT BATTLE

Martial Law Decree Follows Fighting Between Chinese and Japanese Forces

Gen. Sung's Troops Refuse Surrender, Man Walls and Barricade River Banks

TOKYO, July 8. (AP)—A spokesman for the Japanese war office said today Japan will be compelled to take serious action if the Chinese "continue to aggravate"

After her social work education at Columbia University in New York, Clorinda returned home to develop President Franklin Roosevelt's New Deal in Hawai'i.

the full four years to earn a degree in English. Thereafter she worked a year with foreign-born women in the International Office of the Young Women's Christian Association in New York City. Queen Lili'uokalani died in 1917, likely while Clorinda was away. In a pageant that acted out the community's political and social split-mindedness, the Queen was honored with what amounted to a state funeral at 'Iolani Palace and Kawaiaha'o Church. By torchlight, thousands of mourners escorted her casket to the Royal Mausoleum in the uplands of Nu'uanu above Honolulu.

This was the contradictory Hawai'i to which Clorinda returned. She worked for a charitable dental program, then for the Hawaiian Humane Society. There she dedicated herself to the well-being of abused and errant children. She also helped care for Sanford Dole. In his courtly dotage, he had become Gov. Dole and then Judge Dole. In the snobbish Who's Who of the early territory, he was captioned not by office or work but as the Grand Old Man of Hawai'i. When he died in 1926, to Clorinda's surprise she was named the executor of his will.

In the meantime, she had married a land-owning dairyman, Charles Lucas, and given birth to Laura, her only child. She divorced and at age forty, a single mother, made a monumental decision. She moved back to New York with her daughter in tow to study at Columbia University's School of Social Work.

THE NEW DEAL, 1933-1941

The timing of her advanced education was significant, in that it coincided with the federal government's commitment to provide Social Security payments to the poor. This resulted in the reach of the New Deal into America's far islands. With her social work degree in hand, Clorinda became a professional in the territorial government's new Department of Welfare. She interviewed and counseled people, informing them about the financial and emotional support that was becoming available.

She worked under a well-known Native Hawaiian politician, John H. Wilson. His biography by Bob Krauss includes the chapter "Clorinda Lucas and the Welfare Revolt," which describes Clorinda as being more inclined to give orders than to take them. She was bringing social work in Hawai'i "out of the dark ages," establishing welfare not as a charity but an entitlement provided to any person who was eligible due to circumstance. She clashed with Wilson over how much money to give people. Initially, the payment to a family for support of its first dependent child under sixteen was $18 a month and $12 a month for each additional child.[4] While Wilson was out of town,

---

4 Archives of Hawai'i GOV 8-2 memorandum on the administration of Grants in Aid to Dependent Children, Territory of Hawai'i, 6. While the dollar amounts seem pathetic, the guidelines for eligibility were more liberal than the amended criteria enacted six decades later and signed into law by a Democratic president, William J. Clinton, in response to propaganda aimed at "welfare queens." The Territory's memorandum said "children's aid cases are long-time cases, usually for the full school years of the children." Mothers were not expected to be employed outside the home. If they did so, they were supposed to work only part-time and "only such hours and at such times as will not interfere with her proper care of the children." Further, "growing children just out of school should not be expected to assume the full support of the family." If an applicant was denied welfare, she or he could ask for a "fair hearing" by a reviewing official.

Clorinda distributed the agency's cash reserve to the program's beneficiaries. Wilson was outraged but nonetheless stuck with her. He later made her the head of a pioneering social work program that otherwise was populated by women from the US continent. She thought of herself as one who solved social problems, "like psychiatrists in charge of society's behavioral malfunction." She succeeded Wilson as head of the public welfare agency.

CONTINUOUS PERSONAL GROWTH

Social scientists who studied her life discovered an emerging cross-cultural approach to social work and a heightened consciousness of the distinctively difficult experiences of many Native Hawaiians. Clorinda gave talks, delivered papers, and conducted workshops, in which she urged caseworkers to learn about the diversity of the people who applied for welfare.[5] "Lucas took action on behalf of vulnerable children, poor people, and oppressed Hawaiians," the authors wrote. "She confronted and massaged the public welfare system...to provide benefits to which people were entitled. Her social and political power provided her with access to prominent people, while her political astuteness guided her strategies."[6]

"Lucas seemed to have been energized by things that were different, new and even a little scary," the authors went on. "Her career is peppered with examples of adventure, creativity, and gutsiness, which were all qualities that sustained her."[7] She was a founding member of the Hawai'i chapter of the National Association for the Advancement of Colored People and also a founder and the first Polynesian president of the Pan-Pacific Southeast Asian Women's Association.

During World War II, she worked to lessen the suffering of the wives and children of Japanese aliens who had been interned by the US Army's martial law government. She caught the eye of the executive officer of martial law, Col. Thomas H. Greene, who praised her efforts. In 1943,

---

5 LaNey and Main, 302

6 Ibid, 303

7 Ibid, 305

she moved to the territory's Department of Public Instruction, where she became the first director of pupil guidance. At every step of her life-long commitment to the well-being of children, she seemed to see the human condition from an ever more holistic viewpoint.

In the spring of 1946, with the war just ended, she undertook a pil-grimage to deepen her knowledge of student guidance.[8] Her friend and collaborator was a scholar named Mildred Sikkema, then a prominent University of Hawai'i professor engaged in the cross-cultural and interna-tional development of social work. Dr. Sikkema wrote letters of introduc-tion to educators and practitioners across the country. "She is a charming Hawaiian woman," Dr. Sikkema said, "of whom I am most fond." In one letter she added that although Clorinda was a pillar of the community, "She loosens up nicely with a drink or two." Clorinda flew to San Fran-cisco, opening a notebook on the first of her numerous observations. She wrote that pupil guidance—as it then was called—should start in kinder-garten. Further, "Teachers need to be counsellors as well, so as to be con-cerned with the whole child." In addition to teachers and social workers, she conferred with psychologists, psychiatrists, researchers, administra-tors, nurses, and dieticians, foreshadowing a multi-disciplinary approach that eventually would characterize her most important work.

In Pittsburg, she talked with the superintendent of public schools and the dean of the area's school of social work. In Buffalo, she attended a five-day conference on pupil guidance. In Washington, DC, she met with officials of the US Office of Education. She typically took a night train from point to point as a way of stretching her daytime work hours. Often gathering telephone numbers and addresses as she went, she trav-eled on to Baltimore, El Paso, Los Angeles, and elsewhere, sifting ideas and making acquaintances. She returned to Honolulu after two months on the road.

She already was a public figure, but now was in demand for speaking and interviews and her participantion in meetings and panel discussions ticked up further. By the time she retired from the territorial government

8 From Mrs. Lucas's personal notes, uncatalogued Lucas papers, Hawai'i State Archives

in 1960, she was widely known. She was well versed in both the possibilities and limitations of government. She was likewise intimately knowledgeable about Honolulu's private, nonprofit social agencies: Child and Family Service, Catholic Social Services, the Salvation Army, and, most importantly for her purposes, Queen Lili'uokalani Children's Center (QLCC). Freed from the constraints of government, she was named one of the three trustees of the late Queen's estate.

TRANSFORMING QLCC

As with the origins of welfare payments, the timing of Clorinda's new role was auspicious. QLCC then was a small, lightly funded program operating out of a residential house on Miller Street, mauka of 'Iolani Palace. She was QLCC's first female trustee and soon chaired its three-person board of trustees. Among them, Clorinda was the only social worker, which meant she had the most informed ideas and the most specific proposals about how to proceed. The Queen had willed her assets to the protection of "orphans and half-orphans," with a preference to be given to children of Hawaiian ancestry. In the transitional years of Clorinda's tenure, the idea of live-in orphanages had become an anachronism. The trustees successfully petitioned the court for permission to fulfill in a more open-ended way the needs of at-risk children who had lost one or both parents. Predictably, given her background, the inspiration for social work as it had been developed in places like Hull House in Chicago and the Columbia School of Social Work was at the heart of what lay ahead.

Meanwhile, Hawai'i was changing rapidly across many fronts. As mass tourism accelerated, the Queen's landed trust became much more lucrative. Clorinda marveled that the estate at the time of Queen Lili'uokalani's death in 1917 was valued at $135,000 and by the early 1960s was valued at $20 million. With the court's approval, QLCC suddenly had both the latitude and the financial resources to address new and broader definitions of human need.

Pressed lifelong to fit into the haole world, the trustee incarnation of Clorinda found strength in her legacy as a Hawaiian. She thought deeply about the suppression of the Hawaiian language and cultural

Retired after long service to the territorial governent, Clorinda led Queen Lili'uokalani Children's Center into the creation of a bicultural approach to social work.

practices and, more generally, about the Hawaiian people's wounded sense of well-being. Having once said she knew next to nothing about Hawaiian history, in 1967 she delivered a thirteen-page discourse at Kamehameha Schools on the benevolent legacy of King Kalākaua and his queen, Kapi'olani.[9] She was, at the time, chairperson of the school's advisory council. She proudly recounted Kalākaua's fame as the first head of state to travel around the world. She described the splendor of his coronation against the backdrop of the then newly-built 'Iolani Palace. At a time when extant written histories still described the cost of the palace and Kalākaua's coronation as justification for the overthrow of the Kingdom of Hawai'i government, Clorinda spoke of them as markers of greatness. The Hawaiian people, she wrote, returned to their homes with a renewed sense of dignity. She went on to describe Kalākaua's formation of the benevolent society Ho'oululāhui, which was dedicated to shoring up the culture and morale of the Hawaiian nation. Similarly, she celebrated Queen Kapi'olani's support of maternal and infant care programs that became the basis of the Kapi'olani Maternity Hospital.

Clorinda was one of a special few Hawaiians who created a new atmosphere in the 1960s. Her contemporary, John Dominis Holt, wrote in his widely read essay *On Being Hawaiian*: "(We) have been pummeled into accepting the stranger's view of ourselves as being cute, all-abiding, friendly nincompoops, charming and lovable, but certainly inferior as humans—and in need of being looked after by superior beings."[10] He cited Clorinda as one of a handful of role models—"a leader in the field of social sciences"—who people might look to for what he hoped would be a revival of the Hawaiian worldview.

For her part, she said her purpose was to collaborate with individuals dedicated to generating a sense of self-worth among Hawaiians. "And this," she said, "means power in the end, there's no question about that."[11]

9   Thompson family papers

10   Holt, John Dominis, *On Being Hawaiian*, (Honolulu, Topgallant Publishing Co. Ltd., 1974), 9

11   Notes, 4H Alii Award, 1980. Thompson family papers

For her lifetime of social work and her leadership of QLCC, she was the subject of numerous accolades. The National Association of Social Workers declared her a Pioneer. The Hongwanji Buddhist Mission declared her a Living Treasure. The Hawaiian newspaper columnist Sammy Amalu wrote she was one of the grandest women of her era. The genuinely modest Clorinda deflected the attention from herself to her chosen work. "I shouldn't be honored," she said, "for something I enjoyed doing all my life."

Her mother, Lizzie Napolean Low, had died in 1914, when Clorinda was still a teenager. She was buried at Kawaiaha'o Church, where she had attended Sunday School class. Clorinda's father, Eben Low, died in 1954 at age 90. He left instructions that his remains be scattered on top of Mauna Kea on Hawai'i Island, in keeping with Hawaiian tradition. Clorinda was among the mounted riders who ascended the great mountain against the cold and wind, Eben's urn in hand.

She lived on until 1987.

She had set the stage for, and then facilitated, a Native Hawaiian reinvention of social work. Her agent for this transformation was her social worker son-in-law, Myron B. "Pinky" Thompson. Pinky's thinking, she said with unconcealed admiration, was "very different, very new, and very scary for the trustees to even consider." ✦

CHAPTER 2

Ah Quon McElrath

In the way that Clorinda Low Lucas was mainly about healing the historic injustices done to the Hawaiian people, the social work of Ah Quon McElrath was about breaking the grip of the white oligarchy that ran the Hawai'i of her time. Because her labor union identity became so indelible, many people did not realize that she was a social worker. She was—albeit a social worker of a different sort.

In the public shorthand, Ah Quon Leong first became widely known as Ah Quon McElrath of the ILWU—the International Longshore and Warehouse Union—and then simply as AQ. She was born in 1915, making her a full generation younger than Clorinda Lucas. Her parents were immigrants from China who were poor but nonetheless memorable in their own way.

Chew Leong, her father, was from a rice-growing village near where the Pearl River delta empties into the South China Sea. It was one of a cluster of villages in a small area in present-day Guangzhou Province, from which thousands of Chinese departed, driven away by famine and lured to Hawai'i by employment and a story of potential wealth. Chew Leong arrived as a plantation laborer, then quickly left the plantation in search of a way to become his own man. AQ said he worked intermittently. He drove a hack in a time before cars, tried carpentry, and made *ōkolehao* whiskey, which AQ called moonshine. She wondered whether it was the whiskey or the then commonplace smoking of opium that landed her father in Oʻahu Prison. At any rate, he could not have been there for a long term, because he fathered nine children in a period of thirteen years. Of the seven who survived infancy, AQ was the sixth.

In their best times, the Leong family lived together in their own house in Iwilei, which was fabled as the red light district of Honolulu and then as its cannery row, and which today is populated by homeless people.

Ah Quon Leong McElrath (1915-2008) dedicated her life to empowering the working class struggle against the oligarchy that ruled territorial Hawaiʻi. She was a labor radical first, a social worker second.

AQ's Iwilei revolved around the giant, labor-intensive canning plant of the Dole Pineapple Company, the creation of James Dole, cousin of Sanford Dole. Across the street was a can-manufacturing plant where she would eventually attempt to organize the workforce for collective bargaining. There was also a fertilizer company and a series of oil storage tanks next to the harbor. In all, it was a pulsating one-stop, day-night industrial district that defied the image of pastoral Hawaiʻi.

AQ remembered as a small child collecting scraps of lumber to fuel their outdoor cooking stove and metal scraps that she sold to junk dealers. In a gender division of labor, her brothers shined shoes and delivered newspapers. When she was five, her father died. AQ's mother, Shee Wong Leong, suffered from a combination of untreated glaucoma and diabetes. By the time she gave birth to Ah Quon she was blind. By Chinese tradition, her feet had been bound in infancy and sculpted into an imagined delicacy. The pain was nightmarish, and the results were crippling. She tried to take in other people's laundry but could not manage the work, at which point the family broke up and scattered to the shelter of relatives and friends.

Personal grit and jobs for the children in the pineapple industry brought them back together. AQ was to recall to her many interviewers that there were no child labor laws at the time. Children began full-time employment as young as twelve. Driven by the ripening of fruit in the heat of long summer days, the cannery operated day and night. This was conveyer-belt work, run in twelve-hour shifts. An automated coring and peeling device pumped out can-shaped pineapples in an endless stream. AQ was among the white-uniformed women who trimmed the dark little eyes of the fruit with razor-sharp blades. Her starting pay was eighteen cents an hour. After a long apprenticeship, she moved to the cafeteria, where the pay was twenty-seven and one half cents an hour.

The family saved the children's wages, and each fall the children returned to school. Mother Shee Wong devoted herself to the singular cause of their gaining an education. AQ said her mother spoke in "aphorisms," meaning maxims for living. She preached. She resurrected horrors from her childhood in China, when female children were sold and infanticide was not unknown.

AQ experienced the public school system of Honolulu as openminded in ways the plantation system was not. In the seventh grade, a classmate presented a paper on the second five-year plan of the Soviet Union, which then was the shining hope for many communists and socialists. "What an impression that made on me," she was to say. "How is it that a nation can plan its economy and give to and assure each one of its citizens a full, consistent standard of living?"

At McKinley High School, under the well-liked principal Miles Cary, participation in student government was the order of the day. She thought of her teachers as imaginative and expert in their subjects. They spent extra time with her and urged her to excel.

She regarded the study of English as a sort of grail. Her first language was Chinese, and English proficiency was, she said, "a window to the world." She resolved to master it in all aspects, with startling effect. She came to speak with an ease and eloquence that was all her own. One listened to her consciously for incisive content while simultaneously listening for her rich voice and vocabulary. She won a coveted position on the McKinley High School debate team, which traveled to San Francisco to face off with Galileo High School. She wrote well. Beginning in intermediate school she edited the school newspaper, and she went on to write for both her high school and college newspapers.

The family displayed remarkable cohesion, reuniting in a house of their own in an Iwilei neighborhood created by a gas company, which employed one of AQ's older brothers. The neighborhood incorporated about thirty families that she described as Hawaiians, Puerto Ricans, Chinese, Japanese, and Filipinos. People gathered in the evening in a lighted common area, where AQ read to them from the day's newspaper.

As a sensitive student, she was intensely aware of the growing turmoil in the world system. "I went to the University of Hawai'i in the late 1930s during the period of the Spanish Civil War," she was to say. "The cause of the anti-fascist side affected many of us. We felt we had a part because we boycotted Nazi Germany and fascist Italy."[12] She studied sociology, anthropology, political science, and Asian literature. She supported herself with part-time jobs—five at one time in her senior year at UH. With a major in sociology, she became the first Leong to graduate from college.

ORGANIZING LABOR

That AQ found her way to the labor organizer Jack Hall in his early days in Hawai'i is testimony to how closely she was in touch with working people, who then were particularly hard-hit by the country's great economic depression. Hall had run away from home and gone to sea as an angry young teenager. In the ports of Asia, he had witnessed the extremes of dire poverty and colonial privilege, and he had asked himself, "Which side am I on?" He joined the Communist Party on board a ship and dedicated himself to working on behalf of the dispossessed. In 1934, he volunteered to work in the great general strike that shut down

12 ILWU Oral History Project, Part XVII, "Service, Strength and Solidarity," 17 May 2004

AQ McElrath worked closely with labor leader Jack Hall to expand the social safety net and bring economic democracy to Hawai‘i.

not only the West Coast docks but most of the services of San Francisco. In 1935, he jumped ship in Honolulu and began agitating for the organization of workers. He roamed the waterfront, periodically producing a newspaper called *The Voice of Labor*, which he distributed among the sailors and stevedores, the bars and brothels.

AQ, drawing on her newspapering skills, helped Jack Hall with his earliest forays into publishing. In this way, her union organizing and the development of her social work proceeded in parallel.[13]

In 1938, she volunteered to work in the then new public welfare program. The Territory of Hawai'i's plan for implementing the Social Security Act reflected the preliminary nature of professional social work in Hawai'i. It called for the creation of a Department of Social Work, to be led by a director with the master's degree of the sort that Clorinda Lucas had acquired in New York City. Otherwise, the plan noted an acute shortage of social workers and authorized the University of Hawai'i to provide an in-service trainer to begin filling the gap.

Insofar as AQ was initially volunteering, this was either not a real job or an unpaid one, but in the atmosphere of scarcity her sociology courses had gotten her inside the doorway of social work. Eventually she was paid a part-time salary of $75 a month for doing research in a new Department of Research and Statistics, and soon thereafter she gained full-time employment.

True to her colors, she attempted to organize a labor union for social workers. She partially succeeded, although surely not to her liking, in that the workers organized a professional association, not a union. This occurred three decades before public employees began seriously negotiating with the government through collective bargaining.

Like Jack Hall, AQ showed up wherever working people stirred. A combination social, economic, and political movement was forming on a mass scale, led by a small network of labor radicals, among whom she was becoming an integral part. Through Jack Hall she met another organizer, Robert McElrath, a tenacious and outspoken union man. As a student she had her part-time jobs and then her public welfare job, and when Hall and McElrath were hungry she would buy them stew and rice. In 1941, at the age of 26, she married McElrath, to the horror of her mother, who took notice that McElrath was not only haole but

---

13 For the purposes of this chapter, I reviewed and recommend Sanford Zalburg, *A Spark Is Struck, Jack Hall and the ILWU in Hawai'i* (Honolulu, University of Hawai'i Press, 1979); and Dr. Edward Beechert, *Working in Hawai'i* (Honolulu, University of Hawai'i Press, 2008). Zalburg's is more personal, Beechert's more encyclopedic and institutional.

between organizing jobs.

After Japan's bombing of the US Navy base at Pearl Harbor, the labor movement stalled. Prohibited from union activity, the organizers followed martial law regulation for a time without quibble. Hall kept a low profile, working in the Territory of Hawai'i's labor office under the watchful eye of the Federal Bureau of Investigation.

At this stage, the labor movement's modest gains of the prewar period seemingly had been lost. To make matters worse, workers were prohibited by martial law orders from changing jobs without official approval. To do so risked fines and jailing in arbitrary military courts. With the labor market frozen, some employers actually contracted their employees out to other jobs for higher-wage work, then pocketed the markup. For AQ and Bob McElrath, this was particularly outrageous.

In an interview for a short film on martial law, AQ recounted a story about their response. In 1943, a good two years before the end of the war, they went back to organizing. Under the government's nose, they signed up and trained new card-carrying members at the American Can Plant, across the street from where she had worked the cannery line's twelve-hour shifts as child labor. They then began organizing inside the cannery itself.[14]

For income, Bob McElrath worked on the waterfront repairing ships, which gave him entreé into organizing a Marine Engineers and Drydock Workers Association. As part of this effort, Bob and AQ also organized workers at what then was the tuna-packing plant in the Kaka'ako area next to Kewalo Boat Basin. The imagined "one big union" was evolving, a vision based on Marxist analysis to the effect that within the working class one type of work related to another in a ripple effect. Pineapples related to can manufacture, cans to tuna, tuna to boat repairs, boats to drydocking, and so on. This elemental perception was at the heart of the ferocious split that occurred between traditional craft unions, on the one hand, and industrial unions on the other. The common denominator was not the nature of a given job but the solidarity of the working class. Crucially for Hawai'i, this extended to an understanding of

---

14 Interview with author, ca 1994

the shared humanity of all ethnic groups, in contrast to the previous attempts to organize Japanese unions and Filipino unions. AQ believed that their organizing during the war defined "a lot of things that followed with the organizing of the ILWU in Hawai'i at the end of the war on as broad a basis as occurred. People saw what Bob had done and began to ask, 'Why can't we get the same things?'"

A VISION REALIZED

When government restrictions lifted, the membership of the ILWU exploded. In a few short months, a local union of a thousand members became a force nearing 30,000 members. With the ILWU naming Jack Hall as its international director for Hawai'i, Bob McElrath became the director for communication.

How this related to social work became clearer in 1946, when a disastrous tidal wave struck Hilo on Hawai'i Island. The ILWU responded with humanitarian support. Of this AQ said, "I volunteered my services to the union to do the investigations of need, because the entire union was collecting money to give to families that suffered a death or the loss of a home or personal belongings. I also worked with families to get them to understand what it meant to help each other in times of disaster." And then: "This was the prelude to what needed to be done during the long 1946 sugar strike."[15]

The drama of the strike made the headlines, but solidarity in coping with daily life was the back story. The walkout began on Labor Day, September 1, 1946, at which point the union shut down thirty-three sugar plantations, from Hilo to the far west end of Kaua'i. By the standards of today, in which strikes are rare and brief, the ILWU strikes of this period are hard to imagine. They were not only about wages and working conditions but the distribution of power and, with shifts in power, the very nature of society. The strain of having a large part of the labor force out of work and receiving no income was immense. To keep people together, AQ set nutrition guidelines for the union's soup kitchens, counseled families

---

15 ILWU Oral History Project

on keeping their children in school, located income and services for them, and helped them forestall mortgage payments and other forms of debt. The strike lasted seventy-nine days and concluded with a union victory.

The ensuing strike of 1949 was an even tougher proposition. It shut down the docks and, with it, all shipping to and from Hawai'i. AQ was faced with the desperate needs of a more urban and less cohesive population. Once more she supported families by channeling resources and teaching the skills of surviving and coping. The ocean lifeline was closed, and with it the shipping of necessities of all types. Toilet paper became a major topic. In the backlash, large elements of the population joined the owning and managerial class in its opposition to the strike. After six bitter months, more than twice as long as the sugar strike, the union again prevailed.

By this time, the McElraths had two children. A daughter, Gail, was born in 1943, and a son, Brett, was born in 1945. AQ was straightforward about the pressures the children faced. She told them at an early age that she and their father were fighting for a controversial cause, and they were despised in some quarters. An organization called Imua sprang up to agitate against the radical left, spreading conspiracy theories and stoking anymosity. The US House Un-American Activities Committee held hearings in Honolulu, hectoring witnesses and demanding names. Gail referred to herself as a "Red-diaper baby." Beginning in the early grades, some of the children called her Gail McEl*rat* or, in AQ's recollection, "Commie Rat." For recreation, the family would picnic with other families in the labor movement. Some of the children kept their heads down and some not. "I was more of a fight-back person," Gail recalled. The phone would ring and an anonymous caller would spew abuse. "I would say, 'Who the hell are you?' and hang up."

Gail remembered ladling food at soup kitchens. Celebrities who supported labor came and went from their home—the comedian Dick Gregory, the opera singer Paul Robeson, and the folk legend Pete Seeger. Seeger sat on the living room floor with her parents, playing his banjo and making up verses for "Talking Union," which was a sort of rap before rap music existed. What was their verse? No one knows. Perhaps it was this one:

AQ set menus for soup kitchens and guided families in coping with money issues through long weeks and months on strike.

Now, boys, you've come to the hardest time.
The boss will try to bust your picket line.
He'll call out the police, the National Guard,
They'll tell you it's a crime to have a union card.
They'll raid your meetin', they'll hit you on the head,
They'll call every one of you a goddam Red.

At the peak of the Red Scare in Hawai'i, Jack Hall and six others were arrested and charged with sedition under the Smith Act (eventually found unconstitutional). AQ went every day to the famous Bouslog and Symonds law office to transcribe the proceedings.

UNION SOCIAL WORK

From 1938 forward, for most of sixteen years, AQ was a volunteer cohort of an otherwise all-male union leadership. She quit her salaried public welfare job in 1948, and thereafter the union paid her only partially and briefly for special projects. It was not until 1954 that she was hired full-time on salary as senior staff. Uniquely among unions in Hawai'i, she was designated a social worker. She explained, "The union had moved into the area of negotiated medical plans, pension plans, later on dental plans, and a whole slew of social legislation that required the interpretative work of a social worker...the local's leaders realized that a social worker could perform valuable services, including things elected officials could not do.

"As a social worker, I ran an educational program. I talked to members about things they needed to know beyond collective bargaining, like how to access services available from private and public agencies."[16]

In the strikes, she had worked family to family on maintaining people's health. By 1954, the union was negotiating health insurance for its members. She educated workers on their benefits, on the use of medical services, and how to care for the health of their families. She processed medical claims and advocated for members on disputed claims. In so doing, she developed more deeply knowledgeable positions and convictions, which she fed into the union's long-term drive for universal health insurance.

In 1965, at age fifty, she enrolled in a master's degree in social work program at the University of Michigan. The same year, her daughter Gail enrolled in the Case Western University school of social work in Cleveland. The two studied in parallel for a year, then AQ's activism won out over the academic project. She called Gail and told her that she knew more than the professors. She had been wasting time, she said, and now she was heading to the South. Working out of the famous Tuskegee Institute, she settled in Lowndes County, Alabama, a bastion of the Ku Klux Klan and one of the scariest places in all of America.

She lived with a black woman whose house had no toilet and no running water. Where most civil rights volunteers of the time concentrated on voter registration, AQ worked on problems of public health and a clean water supply. So precious was fresh water that after brushing her teeth, AQ was instructed to spit the residue onto the garden plants. She

---

16 Ibid

Although the ILWU was ahead of its time on many fronts, its leadership was traditionally all-male until AQ gradually established a seat at the table.

conducted health screenings by the hundreds. For many impoverished blacks, a medical examination was a novel experience. Most lived on skimpy, unbalanced diets. People unable to afford shoes had tapeworms that entered through their feet and ate away at them. AQ reported that nearly nine of ten impoverished black people were anemic.[17]

She returned to a challenging Hawai'i. The sugar and pineapple industries were being steadily mechanized, requiring fewer workers. Plantations in the less favorable terrains and microclimates were closing. Under these circumstances, the union was bargaining for a percentage of mechanization profits while supporting early retirement and repatriation of Filipinos who wished to return to the Philippines.

As the possibilities of collective bargaining diminished, the public

---

17   Gordon H. Chang, interviewer Judy Young, interviewer and apparent editor; *Chinese American Voices: From Gold Rush to Present* (Berkeley, University of California Press, 2008) 264

sector became ever more important to the ILWU, particularly in the context of its influence over legislators and its close relationship with then Gov. John A. Burns. AQ played an increasingly large role in developing and implementing the union's legislative program, which she regarded as an extension of social work. She testified on and lobbied for human services, public assistance increases, and the ever-present question of health insurance.

ADVOCACY

In 1973, after years of careful groundwork by the ILWU, the State legislature passed the first-ever pre-paid health insurance law. By this time, the union had negotiated health insurance for its membership. Accordingly, from a standpoint of competition among unions to organize new members (in the growing hotel industry, for example), the ILWU insurance plans gave it a strategic advantage. Nonetheless AQ and others advocated for the new law, giving up narrow self-interest for the general well-being of workers.

Along with the Democratic Party, the ILWU was the indispensable force in diminishing the power of the oligarchy and the Big Five corporations that had developed and controlled much of the economy through interlocking directorates. The ILWU was, above all, purposeful. It knew what it wanted. In addition to the widely-known health care law, it was involved in shaping unemployment insurance, worker's compensation, disability insurance, higher workplace safety standards, the development of liberal education in a far-reaching community college system, and support for culture and the arts.

Uniquely among the unions, it employed the practice of social work as one of the ways to build a strong community. One member-service staff member recalled, "If families were strong, the union could be strong. If families fell apart, strikes would fall apart and the union would fall apart."

The ILWU did not lack for effective people of robust social conscience, such as Hall, McElrath, the attorneys Harriet Bouslog, Myer Symonds and Edward Nakamura, and legislators such as the attorney Nadao Yoshinaga and the business agent Yoshito Takamine. In such company, it said a great deal about AQ that she was often described as the conscience of the ILWU.

She helped elevate it. She also changed it from within. Although progressive on class issues, the ILWU was much like the rest of society on gender issues. Other than AQ, the senior leadership was all male. Often impatient, she nonetheless said she realized that many of the members could not be led by a female, but that by her presence and example she helped change that view, relationship by relationship. Now, many years later, the president of ILWU Local 142 is a woman, Donna Domingo.

AQ nominally retired in 1981 at age 65, but actually moved on to a new phase of activism. In the militant union movement, she was the last great figure left standing, and she continued to be an outspoken voice for social justice. Scholars and documentarians gravitated to her for a take on deep history and the challenges of the present and future. The historian Dan Boylan interviewed her dozens of times for documentaries, columns, and the PBS Hawai'i *Island Insights* show. "No one I've ever interviewed possessed AQ's combination of eloquence, commitment, idealism, and pure presence," he recalled. After one particular discussion on health insurance, in which she had not been asked to join, she telephoned him early the next day, beginning with, "Boylan, what's wrong with you?" Of the four panelists, none had advocated for single-payer universal health care. And, she said, "That's the only kind that will work." Boylan loved it: "Just being around her brought out the best in a lot of people."

She remained an unapologetic Marxist throughout her life. Where some of her fellow radicals kept their heads down, fearing their political pasts would be revealed, AQ integrated all the pieces. She advocated openness and dialogue: "By learning our history we can develop new ways in which to enhance our personal lives as well as the collective lives of working people." Looking back at her life's work, she said, "To me this is the story of the awakening of the human spirit through a group called a union."

In the community, thousands of people had been touched by her grace as a social worker. One such young woman had survived a tragic childhood partly thanks to AQ's intervention, then grew up to become a social worker herself. When she happened to meet AQ in her adult role, she was overcome with the recollection of hurt. She burst into tears. AQ held her and whispered, "You are as beautiful as ever."

For some it may have seemed counterintuitive that AQ served on the board of directors of the financially strapped Honolulu Symphony. About the musicians she said, "I do things that I love with people I adore." She played a pivotal role in raising $4 million from the legislature to keep their music going. She advised the board members to double down: "We must get on our hind legs and bay to the moon and say the job is not done."

In 1998, fifty years after receiving her bachelor's degree, she was given an honorary doctorate by her alma mater, the University of Hawai'i. Gov. Benjamin Cayetano appointed her to eight years of service on the Board of Regents (1995-2003), during which time she chaired the Student Affairs Committee and the Academic Affairs Committee. She received numerous other accolades, such as the Pioneer Award of the Asian Pacific American Labor Alliance. Honored at the grassroots People's Fund annual dinner in 2008, she delivered a stern discourse on the evils of economic globalization—this at age 92. She warned that the hard-won influence of organized working people was slipping away in the global arena. She instructed everyone in the room to recruit one additional person to the cause and together they were to tell the world, "We will not take this. Fight back."

She died several weeks later. She left word there was to be no fuss and no funeral. Nonetheless, the ILWU held a remembrance at its union hall attended by several hundred people. Her ashes sat with those of her late husband Robert McElrath, until son Brett died and daughter Gail combined the ashes of all three. Where the waves wash onto Diamond Head, she placed them into the sea. ✦

CHAPTER 3

Myron B. "Pinky" Thompson

Myron Thompson was born on February 29, 1924, the extra day or Leap Day that occurs every four years to realign the human calendar with Earth's journey around the sun. He led the field of social work in Hawai'i down new paths to serve unique circumstances. In the naming of the University of Hawai'i School of Social Work after Thompson in 2008, he was described as a warrior against social injustice. Lifelong, he advocated for justice and healing, influencing people throughout Hawai'i, around the Pacific, and in Washington, DC.

His full name was Myron Bennett Thompson. He was descended from Hawaiian chiefs but had no Hawaiian name. Wrapped at birth in a handy pink blanket, he acquired the nickname Pinky. It stuck, even though its suggestion was entirely inapt. He was a rich brown in complexion, lean, athletic, and full of apparent potential from an early age.

His father was among the more adaptive Hawaiians who had found employment in the newly formed government of the City and County of Honolulu. He worked as a liquor inspector, then became an accountant. Myron's mother taught school. As compassionate guardians of the community, they were social workers of a sort. They took in at-risk young people off the street. Sometimes a dozen were piled up in their house at once, often fresh out of the territory's home for boys who had been judged delinquent. Myron grew up sharing his room and sometimes his bunk. He was to say that in the kind-heartedness of his parents, he first thought about the importance of helping others.

He was the middle of three children. By the year of his birth, 1924, the Hawaiian population of Hawai'i had sunk to a low of 28,000 in the aftermath of the United States' 1898 takeover of Hawai'i. Hawaiian life expectancy was less than forty years. Nonethless, the main subject of public discourse was not what had happened to the Hawaiian people but what might happen if there was a war between Japan and the United States. Pinky Thompson was sixteen when Japan bombed the naval base at Pearl Harbor. He was given a gun and told to guard the beaches against a Japanese invasion. As soon as he had graduated from high school, he talked with a military recruiter. He thought he would like to be an airplane pilot, but the recruiter said someone as dark-complected as he would end up in a mess hall peeling potatoes.

The Army made him an infantry scout, an assignment routinely given to American Indians. It was practically a death warrant. As he and his comrades huddled in a landing craft off France's Normandy coast, a chaplain urged them to pray to their own particular conception of a Supreme Being. Pinky experienced an epiphany. He prayed both to the Christian God and to his Hawaiian 'aumakua, his family's ancestral spirit. He made it past the landing zone and into the Normandy peninsula. There he was shot in the temple by a German sniper but miraculously survived. His head was bandaged during two years of treatment, and then his blinded left eye was covered a long while more. In the darkness of his bandages, he realized what he called "the power of vision"—the central importance of knowing what to do with one's life.

Laid up at a head-wound facility in Maine, Pinky received a long-distance telephone call from his sweetheart, Laura Lucas, daughter of the social worker Clorinda Low Lucas. She wept nonstop through their telephone conversation, then traveled to Maine to support his recovery. The couple had first connected in eighth grade at Punahou School,

*Myron B. "Pinky" Thompson (1924-2003), "the ultimate social worker."
He fundamentally affected social services, health, education, and early
childhood development, as well as revived Native Hawaiian self-respect
through the Polynesian Voyaging Society.*

which had recruited Pinky to play football. On his first day at school he received a note that read, "You're cute. I'm Laura."

Improving slowly, Pinky enrolled in nearby Colby College, where he earned an undergraduate degree. He then earned his master's degree in social work from the University of Hawai'i in 1953. At the time, he was one of about thirty students in the program and likely the only person of Hawaiian ancestry. Thereafter he took a job at the Salvation Army Home for Boys, working with delinquents, runaways, and "incorrigibles"—a term of the day—who were much like the boys he had known growing up in his packed house.

A TURNING POINT

The case of one troubled young man particularly affected him. Pinky racked his brain, trying all the techniques of his social work training but failed to connect. The young man took his own life. Depressed and angry, Pinky decided he did not know enough, that he had to find something more to help people, and that the missing part of his approach was coming to terms with being Hawaiian. He dared to name the crippling truth, which was that Hawaiians were often looked down upon in their own homeland and thereby made to feel inferior. Judging from his repetition of this theme, it was embedded deeply and gnawed at him ceaselessly.

This was in the early 1960s, when the celebration of a one-size-fits-all America was in full swing. The concluding chapter of the influential 1961 book *Hawaii Pono: A Social History*, is titled, "We Are All Haole Now." In James Michener's novel *Hawaii*, the contemporary characters all flourished except the young Native Hawaiian man, who was swept away into the sea by a tidal wave. It was a plot twist on which no one publicly remarked.

LOOK TO THE SOURCE

In this heavily laden environment, Myron was appointed in 1962 to head Queen Lili'uokalani Children's Center, then a small casework agency operating out of a house on Miller Street, mauka of 'Iolani Palace. There he began working on a new approach to tough cases

Myron with his father, left, his mother, right, and his brother and sister. War-wounded, he lived for two years with his eyes bandaged. During this period, he developed what he would call "clarity of vision."

based on his perception that Hawaiian life had been trivialized and distorted. He was convinced that where beliefs and practices had been suppressed, they lived in people's deep memory—even in the absence of conscious understanding or words to express it. The result was pain-filled inner conflict.

Under his aegis, a team was mobilized to address this proposition. It revolved around the consultation of Bishop Museum's Mary Kawena Pukui, a giant of her time who all but single-handedly had preserved and perpetuated numerous strands of the Hawaiian cultural fabric. Mrs. Pukui's counterpart was Dr. Jack Haertig, a psychiatrist of Western training who regarded Hawaiian cultural practices as potentially having great psychological and social value.

Together, they examined perplexing cases brought to them by QLCC social workers, such as Richard and Lynette Paglinawan. The common denominator was the client's lack of response to the then

After apprenticeship as a case worker, Myron made history by advancing bicultural Hawaiian/Western social work as director of Queen Lili'uokalani Children's Center.

extant approaches. The thesis that had influenced both Clorinda Lucas and Pinky Thompson was put to the test in hundeds of cases through many years of rigorous analysis. Each was carefully documented. From this work, three written volumes have been published: *Nānā I Ke Kumu (Look to the Source)* volumes I, II and III. The collective result is a social work movement—more broadly an approach to culture and to the challenges of life—based on research, education, and training.

In this bicultural space, traditional practices such as *hoʻoponopono* (family reconciliation and problem-solving), *lua* (martial training), *lomilomi* (massage) and Hawaiian medicinal remedies have been revived and adapted. Among these openings is a comfortable acknowledgement of family *ʻaumakua*, as when Myron connected with his ancestral figure in the landing craft at Normandy. Now, fifty years since the inception of *Nānā I Ke Kumu*, the work is ongoing.

Coterminously, revenue from Queen Liliʻuokalani's endowment grew rapidly, driven by the economic expansion resulting from statehood. Pinky set out to build new quarters for QLCC. It was not to be just any building but a Hawaiian building, unique in contemporary Honolulu.[18]

I first met Pinky in the building's reception area. Our nominal purpose was the paperwork for QLCC's Head Start classes, which had been organized to serve outlying neighborhoods with large Native Hawaiian populations. Our meeting could have been concluded in a few minutes, but it became Pinky's guided tour of the agency's headquarters.

Everything about it spoke of quality. Its implicit message was not only a welcome but, "You deserve nice surroundings." When clients came in, Pinky said, they quickly felt at home. In a few minutes, he had convinced me of the building's significance. Behind the entryway was a garden courtyard, and in the middle of it a statue of the queen. From this center point, the building had three distinct wings, left, right, and center, forming a Polynesian compound of a sort. The structure was built on a Hawaiian stone platform, as if it were a chief's house.

---

18   As of this writing, Liliʻuokalani Trust has vacated the building and opened a downtown headquarters, reflecting a changed strategy and approach.

Later I was told that when certain trustees wanted to cut corners against mounting cost, Pinky pushed it through by threatening to resign.

STRATEGY AND VISION

During this late 1960s period, QLCC under Pinky's guidance reached into the community through what became known as the Nānākuli Study.[19] The Study was an entering wedge into a more ambitious approach to social work, foreshadowing his use of strategic research and planning. It also reflected his grasp of the fact that the progressive trends in state and federal government would cause new social programs to proliferate. The preamble of the Nānākuli Study said that if social change was to result, "it would be no gain if in this process the Hawaiian lifestyle was destroyed." Rather, innovations in such areas as social services, health, education, and employment should knowledgeably address the potential beneficiaries on their own cultural terms. The study explicitly rejected notions of Nānākuli as "depressed and deprived," "culturally disadvantaged," and "socially disorganized." People could live outside the American middle-class cultural model without being deficient. To this was added, "Biculturalism is both possible and desirable." There was no reason why "the cultural characteristics (including language) now manifest on the leeward coast need to be wiped out in order to increase an individual's ability to get along in the public culture of business, legal matters and politics."

Nānākuli was described as a community that valued relationships over economic gain, and the personal over the impersonal. The study explored patterns of skill development, employment, the meaning of work, and aspirations for the future. Language as a factor in learning and as a feature of identity was analyzed at length. The study also reported on such far-flung subjects as diet, doctoring, dental care, and approaches to education. Infancy, childhood, adolescence, family life

---

19 Ronald Gallimore and Alan Howard, editors, *Studies in a Hawaiian Community, Na Makamaka O Nanakuli*, Department of Anthropology, Bernice P. Bishop Museum, Honolulu, 1968. For premises and organization of the study see pp. 3-8.

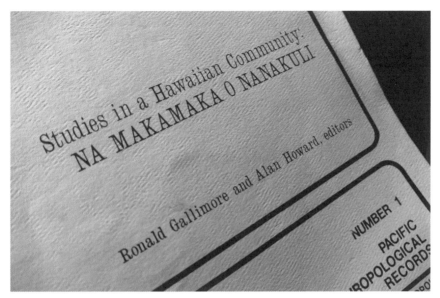

Determined to reach out broadly into the community, Myron Thompson instigated and chaired the Nānākuli Study, addressing the status and condition of Native Hawaiians and laying the groundwork for ambitious innovation in human services.

and community participation likewise came in for fact-gathering and analysis. For the most part, the study stuck to informing service providers with how to more effectively engage with community members. Nonetheless, it took the public school system to task for communicating that for a child to succeed, he or she must become "less Hawaiian."

Without attempting a comprehensive history, the study focused on trends across several generations of Hawaiians. One trend that emerged was the recovery of the combined Hawaiian and part-Hawaiian population, after the extremes of population decline. In fact, people of Native Hawaiian ancestry were Hawai'i's ethnic group with the youngest average sixteen years. With the economy experiencing the statehood boom, the cost of living was rising rapidly—particularly the urban rental market—which in turn drove increasing numbers of low-income Hawaiians to outlying communities such as Nānākuli. The study predicted that without intervention, rapid economic growth would result in further inequality of incomes and rising social resentments. To address this problem, the study proposed development of a culturally-informed skills training and employment program that emphasized cooperation and teamwork—a recommendation that was soon to materialize.

The Nānākuli Study was begun in 1964 and continued for three years. In this window, Pinky made the most of national anti-poverty programs, much as Clorinda had done with the US social security program in the 1930s. In QLCC's hands, the Head Start preschool program became a multi-layered experiment in casework, family healing, and community development. Low-income aides were hired and trained for both classroom and outreach work. Under the direction of the social worker Richard Paglinawan, Volunteers in Service to America were imported, sensitized to the community, and put to work in the field.

IMPACT ON STATE GOVERNMENT

With all of this in motion, Pinky was appointed by the governor, John A. Burns, to chair the state's first Land Use Commission, the statewide classification system that divided all lands of the islands into conservation, agricultural, rural, and urban districts. This was part-time work begun in 1964. The pressure on the first Commission's decision-making was intense. Financial fortunes rose or fell with zoning. Nonetheless, decision-making proceeded with wide agreement, devoid of apparent controversy, under Thompson's chairmanship. This work was no sooner completed than Burns asked him to become the state government's administrative director, a chief of staff position that coordinates the governor's cabinet and serves as the governor's right-hand person. With the right person in place, the administrative director oversees eighteen state government departments and numerous commissions, as well as providing liaison with the state legislature, the four county governments, and the federal government.

Government administration at this level is difficult and cumbersome. Competence matters greatly. Myron Thompson was then forty-three years old. He had clarity of purpose and a rapidly expanding insight into how to make the most of an opportunity. It was often said during this period that Hawai'i was the most liberal and progressive state in

Mr. Thompson with his wife, Laura, daughter of Clorinda Low Lucas, and the influential U.S. Sen. Daniel K. Inouye, with whom Myron worked closely to develop and finance new programs.

the US. Toward this end, Thompson created change and consolidated changes generated by others. Whenever I as a reporter ran across his trail, he was always thinking and acting in terms of reform and innovation. He put his hand on the scale of policy by favoring generous welfare payments, extensions of medical insurance, aggressive public health practices, expanded housing, prison reform, and a healthy environment. When the first Hawaiian civil rights organization, The Hawaiians, arose out of the town of Waimānalo, he ushered a delegation of young and none-too-happy Hawaiians into the governor's conference room to air their grievances and promote their ideas. He also brought in Gov. Burns. "As complaint piled on complaint," I once wrote, "Burns periodically turned to Thompson. 'Is this right?' he would ask. And Thompson would say that it was." Then Burns would ask how the government was to make change.

Pinky spoke his mind plainly. In his hurry, he could be terse, just short of brusque. When he was on the telephone from Washington, DC, his deputy Andrew Chang reported in with a yellow pad, furiously scribbling notes on what was to come next. He telephoned staff and cohorts far into the evening, beginning conversations not with pleasantries but with his latest thinking on how to advance a social agenda.

I once found him fuming, profoundly angry. The legislature was drawing to a close, and he was maneuvering for passage of a bill allowing the state to condemn and take control of the Island of Niʻihau. The goal was to replace its single owner and empower the otherwise all-native Hawaiian population. Within hours of midnight on the last day, the legislature shut the idea down. This had been, in Thompson's view, a chance to break with the feudal and colonial hold of the landowners, and the legislative leadership lacked the vision to execute the idea.

After four years as administrative director, he moved to the Department of Social Services and Housing. One may infer a certain degree of change from the fact that he, a groundbreaking social worker, replaced a former police officer. From there, he went on to serve as director of the Department of Hawaiian Homes, where he oversaw the push of Burns's successor, George R. Ariyoshi, to double the number of dedicated home sites. He also brought his noted protegés, Masaru Oshiro and Richard Paglinawan, into cabinet-level positions in state government, thereby extending the influence of social work in the sphere of policy.

KAMEHAMEHA SCHOOLS

Pinky left state government in 1974 to become one of the five trustees of Bishop Estate, now Kamehameha Schools. The appointment was ground-breaking—for the first time a social worker sat in the boardroom with lawyers, businessmen, and politicians, making policy decisions over hundreds of millions, and eventually billions, of dollars. Again, the timing was right. The 1960s Great Society initiative of the US government was in retreat, but Thompson now had a say in one of the most endowed institutions in the country. He led Bishop Estate from its sole preoccupation with its Kapālama campus above Honolulu into a broader concern for Hawaiian neighborhoods throughout the islands. His focus was on the child from conception to school level, intellectually in the tradition of Clorinda Lucas and the findings of the Nānākuli Study. Spurred by his leadership, the estate supported maternal health clinics, infant care, pre-preschool programs, hearing programs (a widespread problem resulting from untreated early childhood ear infections), and a collaborative participation with other providers in widening the reach of preschools.

In addition to his direct impact on Kamehameha Schools, he orchestrated the development of programs with the federal government that over the years were to bring hundreds of millions of dollars to Hawai'i.

He became a trustee of Bishop Estate (now Kamehameha Schools), where he focused on child development from infancy through preschool.

This happened in three steps. The first picked up on the view, first articulated in the Nānākuli Study, that Hawaiians were not benefiting proportionately from Hawai'i's post-statehood economic expansion. Thompson now chaired a needs assessment, partnering with social justice advocates such as the labor attorney Alvin Shim, the Native Hawaiian community leader Winona Rubin, and the social worker James Bacon. The result was the employment training agency, Alu Like, meaning "striving together." Alu Like continues today, having provided skills development and employment placement to more than 100,000 people.

His second federal initiative was in education. Here Thompson instigated and then chaired a fact-finding group appointed by the US Secretary of Education. The approach to fact-finding followed much the same strategy as Alu Like but went deeper. It included a straightforward recounting of the issues of history, reaching back to incursions and invasions by Western powers that culminated in the 1898 American takeover of the independent Kingdom of Hawai'i. "Since Cook landed, there have been a lot of putdowns for Hawaiians, and you still see the [effects] today," he told the US Congress. "Where does it get started? At birth. In the family."

"We Hawaiians are an enigma," he testified. "We are fascinated by our history, though much of it is nightmarish. We are a compassionate people, fiercely proud of our cultural heritage..." to which he added, "and we are outraged to see our fragile physical setting—our tropical waters, mountains, air, flora and fauna being polluted and trampled to death by civilian in-migrants." The resulting Native Hawaiian Education Act continues to bring in tens of millions of dollars a year to the educational systems of Hawai'i.

The third initiative was health care, spelling out what everyone knew—that the health profile of Native Hawaiians was significantly worse than most people's in Hawai'i and across the country. The road to improvement seemed especially hazardous, in that Congress had never agreed on a national approach to health care. Added to this was a tangle of public and private providers, as well as Western, Hawaiian, and culturally hybrid practitioners. It was against this ongoing disarray that Thompson worked to bring a level of bicultural integration to health care. As before, he organized people around the idea of bringing Hawaiian culture into the light and drawing on its strengths. The assessment brought to the forefront the brilliant contributions of Dr. Kekuni Blaisdell, then a professor of medicine at UH's John A. Burns School of Medicine, and a growing group of Native Hawaiian doctors—such as Dr. Ben Young and Dr. Naleen Andrade—whose work spanned Hawaiian and Western practice. To coordinate such diverse elements, Thompson led the formation of Papa Ola Lōkahi, a culturally informed Native Hawaiian health agency. Through this agency, again, tens of millions of federal dollars flow into programs in Hawai'i annually through the Native Hawaiian Health Act.

In creating these programs, Pinky collaborated closely with US Sen. Daniel K. Inouye and traveled frequently to Washington, DC, to give what was always the lead testimony of Hawai'i to congressional committees.

Always the social worker, Pinky did not advertise himself. If a few people knew of his work in one area, they might not know of his work in a related one. At a community level, he was the capable presence who, at close range, would carefully explain why certain undertakings were important, and that mitigating the historic wrongs done to Native Hawaiians benefited society as a whole. Being a trustee of Bishop Estate had moved him up the income scale, but he drove around Honolulu in a small jeep-like SUV. He avoided social clubs. At a party at the Thompson compound, he would stand in the back of the singers and the guitar players, strumming his home-made bass, which was a galvanized wash tub with a recycled neck and a set of strings. He attended his grandchildren's kayak races. He became a paddler in the senior men's division of the Hui Nalu Canoe Club, which his illustrious ancestor Duke Kahanamoku had co-founded a century prior as a kind of last gasp effort to save Hawaiian water sports.

POLYNESIAN VOYAGING

His subtlest contribution—some would argue his most important—had to do with a canoe. He had been an original supporter of the Polynesian Voyaging Society (PVS). From the perspective of his social work agenda, the voyaging society's revival of Polynesian canoe-building and non-instrument navigation connected Hawaiians to epic achievement. It offset the negative stereotypes, and it generated a combination of awe and intense pride.

The first voyage was in 1976, the year of the Alu Like startup. The double-hulled *Hōkūle'a* was sailed to Tahiti and back, substantially dispelling the widely held view that the Polynesian Pacific had been settled by a series of hit-or-miss accidents. That pioneering voyage confirmed the theory that the peopling of the great Polynesian triangle, reaching from Hawai'i in the north to Aotearoa (New Zealand) in the southwest to Rapanui (Easter Island) in the southeast, had been purposeful, knowledge-driven and skill-based. *Hōkūle'a* was greeted in Tahiti and on its return to Hawai'i by tens of thousands of people who, from a single experiment, now had an expanded view of what it meant to be Hawaiian.

Nonetheless, the successes of 1976 were qualified. The navigator was not Hawaiian but a Micronesian, Mau Piailug, from remote Satawal atoll, where non-instrument canoe navigation had survived the cultural erosions of modernity. In addition, there had been a smudge of negative publicity resulting from an onboard fist fight that had broken out as the canoe neared Tahiti.

A second voyage set out in 1978 with an implied mission of perfecting the record. Instead, it failed. Five hours out, the canoe was caught in heavy seas and capsized. The celebrated lifeguard of O'ahu's North Shore, Eddie Aikau, was part of the crew. He attempted to contact rescuers by making landfall on a surfboard but was lost at sea. Finger-pointing followed over preparation, training, and safety standards. The results were devastating. It was as if the demons of negativity that haunted the Hawaiian narrative had won out.

Myron's son Nainoa, one of the original crew members, would recall, "There was no vision. There were no dreams. There was no hope. It was all replaced with shame and guilt and pain, sorrow, and anger." It seemed likely that the initiative of Polynesian voyaging was at an end. At this lowest of low points, Myron Thompson stepped in. He rallied the 'ohana of the canoe and set PVS back on course. (Technically, he was chairman of the board of directors.) Nainoa Thompson became the student of the navigator Mau Piailug, who was induced to return from Micronesia to Hawai'i as a trainer and teacher. While Myron regrouped PVS, Nainoa studied astronomy and non-instrument navigation. The Hawaiian blessing of the crew on its next departure was, "E aloha kekahi i kekahi a e momoe aku imua." *Love one another and push ahead with determination.*

With careful preparation and execution, the voyage of 1980 achieved its goals flawlessly. As the first Hawaiian non-instrument navigator in contemporary time, Nainoa Thompson became the much-celebrated face of *Hōkūle'a*, but he thought of his father as the irreplaceable moving force: "He navigates us out of the deepest, most painful place, and he brings not just hope. He creates success." Chad Babayan, a second Hawaiian navigator, described Myron similarly: "Spiritually, we were very wounded... He showed us we had to rebuild ourselves." Unintentionally, these were

Arguably Thompson's greatest contribution to the well-being of the community was his leadership of the Polynesian Voyaging Society and its famous canoe, Hōkūleʻa.

words that might be used to describe a skilled social worker.

The impact of *Hokūle'a* is as widely assumed as it is incalculable. The Native Hawaiian political science professor Dr. Noelani Goodyear-Ka'ōpua wrote: "For Kanaka throughout Hawai'i, it represented a sort of undeniable, in-your-face redemption against the racist narrative saturating daily life, including especially those taught in schools. Its success spoke back to systems and individuals who demeaned and discounted Native knowledge (and people) as worthless, feeble, and anachronistic."[20] Success has followed success, as Hawai'i's sailors and navigators have voyaged around Polynesia, around the Pacific and, most recently, around the Earth.

Pinky's son-in-law, Bruce Blankenfeld, said that prior to Pinky and all the many others who drove the Hawaiian renaissance, "Hawaiian culture *was...* [Now] Hawaiian culture *is.*"

Myron Thompson constantly evolved but never wavered from his core theme—that Hawaiians must be free to be Hawaiian, thus enabling them to make a special contribution to, and succeed in, the wider world. This meant spanning both. Thompson's own practice of working in two worlds was astonishing. While organizing *Nānā I Ke Kumu*, he had chaired the first Land Use Commission and then served as number-two man to Gov. Burns in the state government. While driving the formulation of enduring social, health, and education legislation through the US Congress, he had navigated the revival of Polynesian voyaging.

He influenced politics but never played the politics of influence-peddling. He was on close terms with US Senator Daniel K. Inouye and through this relationship a committee emerged with the goal of electing a Native Hawaiian governor, which was a first inkling that such a thing might be possible. The committee chairman was Pinky Thompson. By 1986, a young labor lawyer, John David Waihe'e, was governor, following George R. Ariyoshi. Waihe'e recalled: "Pinky worked not just on Native Hawaiians. He worked on creating a forest of people who under-

20   Dr. Noelani Goodyear-Ka`ōpua, *The Seeds We Planted*, (2013, Minneapolis, University of Minnesota Press), 173

stand Hawai'i. I've been in meetings where Pinky is there, and Senator Inouye is there and, my boss at the time, the labor attorney Alvin Shim, is there. And you knew whatever the issue was, whether you agreed with it or disagreed with it, Pinky was coming from a place of unselfishness.

"So," Waihe'e continued, "you could trust Pinky at an unusual level, what I call 'trust plus.' There are different kinds of trust. Certain people you can trust to be loyal, for example, and there are people you can trust to be competent. And then there is another level where you can trust that somebody really, actually, has the greater good at stake. And Pinky had all three."

Myron Thompson's energy for social justice never waned. He never grew old. In conversation, he wanted most to talk about how to make the world a better place. He believed the ideas were working. He believed the power of vision was working. He passed away on Christmas Day, 2001, at the age of seventy-seven, from cancer, to the surprise of the many who subconsciously felt that a person of such vitality would always be with us.

The National Institute of Health endowed a Myron Thompson chair at the John A. Burns School of Medicine. The old frame building of the health consortium Papa Ola Lōkahi was renamed the Pinky Thompson Building. When the UH School of Social Work was named for him, students composed a chant honoring his life story. It invoked the deity of the ocean, Kanaloa. It invoked the backbone of the land (*iwikuamo'o*). And then, in Hawaiian,

> *Fed by the elder,*
> *the younger retains the knowledge*
> *Bud forth and grow,*
> *Increase and thrive*
> *To live a full life,*
> *Long live the Nation.* ✦

PART II

Personal Stories

With unanimity in our work group on the choices available, I interviewed five living social workers who functioned as agents of social change. The interviews lasted several hours, often with follow-ups. Sometimes a member of our group sat in and, at a certain point, chimed in with a question or a point. All in all, we were taken by the freshness and frankness of our subjects' storytelling styles. They brought to life a process of constantly becoming.

We were reminded that to become a social worker is to embark on a journey of self-discovery and self-development.

The result is a Part II that is substantially in the words of pioneers in social justice work. Where apt, their statements are presented in the style of books created by the UH Oral History Center founders Warren and Michie Nishimoto, and more remotely by the Chicago talk-radio celebrant of human diversity, Studs Terkel. The interviews have been edited for length, with nips and tucks for purposes of clarity and continuity. For example, if someone referred to "the school in the '70s," it might more precisely become "the School of Social Work during the 1970s."

As their stories evolved, they began to intersect, a reminder that Hawai'i still has a small-town quality, and that on islands there is a tendency for everyone to know everyone. Ideas travel quickly.

CHAPTER 4

Masaru Oshiro

Among the social workers who deeply impacted Hawaiʻi, none followed so closely in the steps of Myron Thompson as Masaru Oshiro, albeit from different origins. His story is about personal growth and high achievement through social work. At a young age, Masaru experienced injustice first-hand when his family was ejected from their farm as Japanese Americans in the aftermath of Japan's bombing of Pearl Harbor. He was shy. He was reluctant to speak up. He saw himself as less capable than more articulate people. Nonetheless, he struggled to find justice for his family and express himself while helping others.

Nudged along by the social justice movement of the 1960s and 1970s, he rose to prominence as a social worker. At a time of experimentation, he succeeded Thompson as director of Queen Liliʻuokalani Children's Center.

Without intending to become involved in politics, he became entwined with Congresswoman Patsy T. Mink, with one-time lieutenant governor Thomas P. Gill, and with two governors, John A. Burns and George R. Ariyoshi. He played important roles in the top reaches of state government. As a deputy director of the State Corrections Division, he was asked to endorse capital punishment for "cop killers." Rather than comply, he resigned from his job. As his dissenting view played out publicly, his quiet voice became a moral voice. To this day, Hawai'i does not have capital punishment.

Question: *Is there a place you would like to begin? First things first?*

Masaru Oshiro: I was born in the plantation town of Waipahu in 1928. I thought of it as limited. Most people only went to school until the eighth grade. If there was ambition to go on, the student had to go to Honolulu, to Farrington [High School] or McKinley. As we were going up through the grades, Waipahu High School opened, and that was a lift. Also, with four sisters I was the family's only son, which in Japanese tradition gave me a little privilege.

This was during the Great Depression. In the plantation community, the mark of boyhood or manhood was measured by athletic proficiency. I was very much intrigued by my dad's storytelling of the karate prowess of his dad and other Okinawan disciples of the martial arts. The samurai heroes depicted in Japanese movies prompted me to read about them in Japanese books and magazines, and even today the code of the samurai is subtly embedded in my mode of behavior. Boxing, football (starting with barefoot football), and baseball were also popular, and I immersed myself in all of them.

Dad worked as a truck driver for O'ahu Sugar Company, and my mom worked in the pineapple cannery. Dad and his brother bought four acres of land near Pearl Harbor that was covered with kiawe brush and lantana and coral rock. Over two years, we clawed away at the land, remaking it into a farm. We actually dug a water well with pick and shovel. We built a piggery that was first rate and we began growing beans and cabbage. For my parents these were times of great excitement and expectation.

Everything changed on December 7, 1941. My parents left home early to work on the farm, and they became eyewitnesses to the attack. Because the farm was outside Pearl Harbor's main gate, they were shut

Masaru Oshiro, born in 1928, first served as a caseworker under Myron Thompson, then suceeded him as director of QLCC. There he nurtured QLCC's path-finding intercultural project, Nānā I Ke Kumu. He touched the conscience of Hawai'i by his principled opposition to capital punishment.

out of their hard-earned place. Pearl Harbor, December 7—that was a combat zone. The military needed a buffer, and my parents were chased out of there. The land was confiscated. My father was forced to sell off our pigs. I was thirteen. So there was a kind of emotional loss and anger at the government.

For three years, 1943 to 1945, I lived in the mountains with an "ag" teacher, five of us. We slept on the floor in an old bunkhouse. Our teacher brought in piglets, and we got them up big enough to go to the market— which was the plantation store in Waipahu. We learned a lot, taking care of the pigs, cooking, doing the chores, doing carpentry, and driving an old truck over the mountain roads—all the while keeping up our studies at Waipahu High School. I gave my share of the earnings to my parents, except for an allowance and money to buy war bonds, which everyone was encouraged to do. The summer of 1945, I got a job as a truck helper. My ID badge said RESTRICTED, a racist policy that meant we could not go on a military base. It was the summer the war ended, and it was a time of questioning and aimlessness and drinking beer with friends.

The Japanese American 442nd (Regimental Combat Team) organized midway through the war, and they were my heroes. I followed their example and volunteered for the US Army. I was sent to Japan in the Occupation. We arrived in Yokohama in December in the brutal cold—rumpled, with towels around our neck, trying to stay warm! We weren't what the Japanese people expected of Americans. Ethnically, the Occupation force consisted of haoles, blacks, "pachukos" (Mexican Americans) and, as we were called, "the local boys."

Initially we engaged in serious combat training, with the understanding that we were to counter any aggression by Communist forces. Then we local boys were pulled out of our units and scattered throughout Japan. I was assigned to a three-person team in a remote area where I doubt an American soldier had ever been. The country was swimming with Japanese soldiers returning from abroad. They really didn't want to be identified as soldiers, but they wore tattered uniforms as the only clothes protecting them from the winter. There were children everywhere, begging us for candy and gum and cigarettes, which the Army gave us as handouts.

Masaru Oshiro encountered injustice as a teenager when his family was barred from its Oʻahu farm following Japan's bombing of Pearl Harbor. Inspired by the Japanese American 442nd Regimental Combat Team, he served in Occupation Japan, where he witnessed massive human suffering.

Our job was to monitor Japan's first [postwar] election in 1947. We were instructed to get names of Communist participants. Not reading Japanese, we really didn't know, but Japanese officials were eager to share names.

I tried to get a leave to search for my relatives on Okinawa. My request was denied but eventually—over four decades later, in 1996—I went with my wife Kiyoko and learned that most of my family had been killed in the Battle of Okinawa. They fled the battle scene and hid in caves, where Japanese officers took their own lives, and in despair they went home with the fatalistic idea that if they were to die they would die in their village.

Q: *And how did you get from the Army to studying social work?*

Masaru: I was fortunate. When I got my discharge and returned to Oʻahu, I had the support of the GI Bill, free books, tuition, and a check for seventy-five dollars a month. I enrolled in the University of Hawaiʻi, and I was really lucky because I found mentors who became friends. The first one was Kiyoshi Ikeda (later a distinguished professor of sociology at UH), my friend from Waipahu High School. Kiyoshi was my lifeline. He had military experience, which I had, and he helped me open up to the whole field of social service. He introduced me to new ideas and served as my big brother. Sometimes I stayed with him in the dorm. We were the same age, but he was an upperclassman, and it was partly from his influence that I thought about social work. I finished my undergraduate degree in 1952 and enrolled in the two-year MSW (master's in social work) program.

One of my major influences on the faculty was Mildred Sikkema. I was pretty mediocre academically, but Dr. Sikkema somehow saw things in me she liked. I knew that I was nowhere close to my other classmates, who seemed to know so much more for whatever reason. And my personality caused me to hold myself back. I always hold back. I'm always the one that somebody has to reach out to and say, "Masaru, you haven't said anything." You have to ask me.

Dr. Sikkema convinced me that professional social work was my field. She said, "Even if you're shy, it doesn't matter. If you're helping the person, that person is so preoccupied with self, they don't care what kind of personal approach you have."

Q: *Why was it such a struggle to speak up?*

Masaru: I'm generally an introvert. I'm not the one to lead conversations, lead discussion, or try to express an opinion and defend it. I never felt I'm superior to anybody, and in fact I always felt that the next person is better than me. The other person knows more. Maybe it has to do with the other person being a little more articulate. It took me many, many years to realize that being articulate does not necessarily mean the person knows more. And as life goes on, you find out that, oh, perhaps that guy's more talk than anything else. But in the beginning, you don't know these things.

My first job was as a caseworker at Child and Family Service. You're the new person coming in and you know your role. You're the freshman. You keep your mouth shut. That's the local style. Don't try to stick your head up. Don't try to talk to show that you're not afraid. Well, I played my role as the person who's new, who doesn't know anything. "I'm here to learn."

I can tell you when I started changing. [My wife] Kiyoko and I left Hawai'i for Los Angeles. We were there about a year and a half. She pursued her studies in education, and I worked at a Veterans Administration outpatient clinic. Half of the crew were Black. The rest were haoles. My supervisor happened to be a Japanese American from California, and—very fortunate—she and I clicked. You know that mainland Japanese Americans are very competitive, very articulate. They speak good English. For us, more the local, I feel more comfortable talking to people who are talking local. It took me maybe half a year until I began to hold my own. Even if they said, "Masaru, you have a good case to present. Why don't you present your case?" I would find ten reasons why I can't present.

In group supervision, we talked about veterans struggling with rehabilitation problems and disability problems. As I listened, my goodness,

I begin to think I can compete as a social work clinician. I'm realizing I can hold my own. So I started volunteering.

COMING HOME

Masaru: When we came back, Hawai'i was already the fiftieth state. My heroes, the 442nd veterans, had finished college. They'd gone into law school, and they were getting involved in politics. Many of them—the Dan Inouyes, the Spark Matsunagas—moved right into power positions.

The farm owners got together, trying to get our family land back from the government. A friend of mine took the lead, and he asked me to be the secretary-treasurer. So we were the leadership among the ex-farmers. The tie to politics was fairly easy. We had Dan Inouye in Washington, DC, and Hiram Fong, and Tom Gill, but we found out they couldn't do anything. Of course, years later I realized they had just gotten elected. No seniority. What were they in Washington? They couldn't help us.

Q: *You were never compensated for your family land?*

Masaru: That's the short story. The land went out to public bid and we came out fourth best. Eventually, the government did pay us $2,000, $3,000 for a four-acre property. That was the end. Campbell High School is there now.

Meanwhile, Patsy Mink was living in Waipahu, and we were living in Nānākuli. Before you know it, my wife Kiyoko and I were involved in Patsy's campaign [for Congress]. From then on, Kiyoko and I were her diehard supporters. We grew up with her strong liberal views about many things in Hawai'i, even to the extent of fighting with the Burns administration when the Burns power group was, you know, separate from hers. It was uncomfortable at times, because a lot of my friends were already with the Burns faction, but we were mostly with Patsy Mink—Patsy and Tom Gill.

CASE WORK

For the next three years, Masaru worked as a psychiatric social worker for the

Masaru Oshiro with Gov. John A. Burns, who named him to chair the State of Hawai'i parole board.

State of Hawai'i. He brought an intense commitment to his clients—what some saw as an "unprofessional" level of commitment.

Masaru: I violated some of the basic ideas of what a professional social worker is. In traditional social work, you don't get involved with families that closely. In disaster work, you don't give out your home phone number. I differ. I believe you're in a helping profession. You make a commitment when you have a client. When they need to call you, they've got to be able to call you. Every one of my clients gets my home phone number. If they forget my number, it's in the phone book. I deal with their situation the best I can over the phone. If I cannot, I go over to their house or they come over to my house.

This one boy called me, a runaway. I tell him, "I want you to go back to Detention Home, or if you're brave enough to catch a bus and come to 'Aiea, I'll pick you up." So I pick him up and his girlfriend is with him. It must have been about eleven o'clock or so and there's no more bus. I'm not going to take them back to town, so he and the girlfriend come over [to my home]. I say, "Tomorrow morning, she goes back to school. If you run away, I have to call the police. Up to you. I won't be holding you."

Masaru caught the eye of Pinky Thompson, director of what was then a small agency, Queen Lili'uokalani Children's Center.

Masaru: I worked closely with Pinky, throwing around wild ideas about what we can do to help Hawaiian children. That was the theme. We would put everything on the table. Our (Hawaiian) culture committee got started. We moved into our new building, very proud of what it was going to do. When federal money became available through the War on Poverty, we tapped it. He had no qualms about using non-professionals, community people, to help Hawaiian kids. We went into the schools, into pre-internship programs, trying to get more Hawaiians into the helping professions.

Then the VISTA (Volunteers in Service to America) program opened up, allowing mainland kids to come to Hawai'i to work in poverty communities. Pinky said, "Go for it." In community work, we didn't limit our services to only Hawaiians. Whoever lived in Nānākuli; whoever lived in Moloka'i; whoever lived in Kahuku, Hale'iwa—now we're working with community. By working with community, the Hawaiian kids were going to benefit. Kate Stanley (later a state representative and policy advisor to the governor) was one of the first volunteers to join us and remain with us in Hawai'i.

OPEN DOOR

Masaru: There was a feeling that everything was happening at QLCC. Not only Hawaiian but non-Hawaiian. Change was emanating from the Children's Center. The doorway was open to all kinds of activities.

We opened the conference room to use by the Native Hawaiian grass-roots movement. Soli Niheu? You know that name?

Q: *Very definitely.*

Masaru: Pinky had formed an advisory council of people from the community—business, medical, education—but we didn't have anybody from the grassroots. So we agreed on inviting Soli into the council. Soli became a well-known activist through the first big community protest of that time, which was supporting local famers against eviction for the development of Hawai'i Kai. That was Kalama Valley.

I told staff, "Get out there and see how Queen Lili'uokalani Children's Center can be of help." Around this time, people like Steve Morse and Palani (Francis Kauhane) worked with us, and the famous George Helm was in and out.[21] My attitude was, "There are many things we cannot do, but we won't know until you start talking." So they all went. Three or four families could use our help immediately. They needed supplemental financial assistance. Some kids were already having trouble in school, so the staff workers took them all in. Here again, different things were happening and we were able to respond. I always said the future of social work is terrific because a private agency can do these things with the right kind of leadership.

Pinky wanted QLCC to go to Moloka'i because that's what the Queen had wanted. Serve the children of Hawai'i, not just the children of O'ahu. Serve children all over. Hawaiian children. Destitute children. I recommended Tom Tizard (a senior social worker interested in community organization) and Pinky said, "Okay. I trust his instincts." We didn't have an office on Moloka'i, but Tom says, "No problem. I'm going to move there with my wife and kids." Just rent a place and oper-

---

21 Steve Morse: both a social worker and a creative writer, subsequently active in the protests of the bombing of Kaho'olawe and staffing for development of the Native Hawaiian rights amendments of 1978 to the State Constitution; Francis Kauhane, similarly, a social worker, activist and contributor to the Constitution; George Helm, activist, singer, poet, spiritual leader of the Kaho'olawe movement, lost at sea during an access trip to the island

ate from there. That was the beginning of what is now the QLCC programs all over Hawai'i.

Q: *What enabled Pinky to move forward with such confidence?*

Masaru: It's natural for him to relate to different levels of people. He was able to relate to everyone from kids all the way up to the highest politicians. He's not confrontational. He listens. He will not challenge you right away if he does not agree with you. You know, in social work, you go where the other person is first.

He told all of us senior administrators, "Get out into the community." He didn't want us to be in the office running our little empires. He wanted us out there, so I put my name in for non-paid service on a state board.

Soon after that, parolees killed two police officers in a supermarket robbery. It caused a tremendous uproar over parole, and it gave Gov. Burns an opening to appoint a new board. He called me into his office, which then was at 'Iolani Palace, and he said, "Masaru, you're going to be chairman of the board." I was [only a young social worker], and I said, "You're kidding. I'll just be a board member." I was shocked. I had no experience with public service or law violators, but he was not about to take no for an answer. The governor says, "Look at your fellow board members." There were two union representatives, a schoolteacher, and the manager of a catering business. He said he wanted someone attuned to behavioral problems, and that was me, the social worker. How do you say no to the governor after that?

There was an ongoing clash between the tradition of punishment and the more compassionate or optimistic view of rehabilitating criminal offenders. I of course represented rehabilitation. I remained in touch with parolee support organizations, such as the John Howard Association, as well as religious interests that advocated for community correction centers. It may seem amazing today that we had only three hundred or so male prisoners and a small handful of female prisoners. This is in contrast to the present, in which the jails and prisons are overflowing and Hawai'i's people are being shipped off to mainland prisons, away from their families and communities. This is far from how I envisioned our system should be.

In this same period, I was chairman of NASW (National Association of Social Workers/Hawai'i Chapter). We didn't have staff, so [my wife] Kiyoko wrote the newsletter. We set up an NASW office at QLCC, and for a time QLCC became the center of NASW activity. Nobody could say QLCC worked in isolation. In fact, one of the most respected people in the field said to me, "Masaru, you know, QLCC is the mecca of social work."

HOLDING THE FORT

When we moved to our new building on Halona Street, Pinky said, "I'm going to have you be social work director." He just created a new position. He doesn't even talk about organizational structure. Pinky doesn't worry about things like that. He says, "You, you're going to be in charge."

Gov. Burns already knew enough about Pinky to trust him to take on a big job—the first chairman of the Land Use Commission, dividing up the whole state into what shall be conservation, agriculture, urban, all that. Then Gov. Burns asked him to become his Administrative Director. When Pinky told me I said, "That's a big jump from Queen Lili'uokalani Children's Center." But Pinky said, "I got to go." He says, "Can you hold the fort?" I knew we had to have a Hawaiian be the director, and I was not. But serving as interim, that was okay. Within a few months, trustees called me in to say, "Masaru, you're doing the job. Just take it." So I became the executive director. I was there for seven years. (Chuckles.)

I owe it to Pinky. I owe it to QLCC for giving me the opportunity. I brought every skill and all the energy I had to that job. I read Queen Lili'uokalani's *Hawai'i's Story*, and I identified with her struggles. I saw the brilliance of what she did as a leader in a struggle that she never won. I said, "Hey, everybody should be reading this book to see where we are in Hawai'i." I read many other things about history, the overthrow, even to the point of learning about the anti-statehood factions.

People started saying, "You sure you're not part Hawaiian?" I'm not totally Japanese, but I'm Okinawan, which is an identification I grew up with. To be Okinawan was a proud thing to be. So, too, was being part-Hawaiian.

Q: *All the while, QLCC was researching and retrieving Hawaiian culture.*

Masaru: Richard Paglinawan was the lead in many ways. I had the privilege of being Richard's first supervisor when we were at Young Street. All the rough kids, the ones we got referred from Detention Home, I said, "Richard, another one. Get over there." He had a full caseload of young, acting-out types. Every now and then, these kids would run away. Richard wanted to know, "Do I grab them before they get out of the office?" He was a McKinley High football player, also judo and even Hawaiian *lua* (warrior). I tell him they are running because they have a great need to avoid whatever situation they're in. "If we have to call the police, we're going to have to call the police. But you will not chase runaway kids. When they're ready, they'll come back if they think you are sincere."

Q: *Richard presented the case that got the cultural committee going?*

Masaru: A young boy felt his family was cursed—felt that he's going to die before he becomes an adult. I didn't know how to help. The negative connotation of a *kahuna* was prevalent among most people at that time. And I'm not even talking about social workers. It was the whole community. When you say "*kahuna*," it's like throwing a curse. It's shooting bad luck against a person you don't like. It's negative.

My job was to reach out to Dr. Haertig (psychiatrist). From there we needed a cultural anthropologist. I didn't know a person by the name of Mary Pukui then. But Richard had studied archaeology at UH before he studied social work—and I think he must have gone to Bishop Museum or to Mrs. Pukui's house.

Through our discussions with Mrs. Pukui and Dr. Haertig, suddenly, "kahuna" was a neutral term. A kahuna is a priest or an expert in an area of the culture. There is a kahuna for canoe building, a kahuna for herbal medicine, and so on. This frees us to explore other cultural areas. How do you solve interpersonal conflict? Interfamilial conflicts or village conflicts? We were unearthing Hawaiian healing practices.

NĀNĀ I KE KUMU

Masaru: Everything just fell into place. Before you know it, Mrs. Pukui started coming weekly. Jack Haertig came weekly. He would take the lead. He had a tremendous respect for Hawaiian practices, and he knew human behavior. He could see all the connections—the value of the ethnocultural aspects of things. Richard and his wife Lynette brought up the cases with the deepest questions about Hawaiian culture. In this sense they became the driving spirit.

The QLCC Culture Committee evolved into a force of historic importance. Mrs. Pukui was a taproot into what was by then a waning Hawaiian culture and a disappearing language. The least predictable addition to the committee was Malia Craver, a native Hawaiian speaker with a deep cultural background.

Masaru: Malia was an aide, non-college. Pinky had known her as a house mother at the Salvation Army Boys home in Kaimukī, and he hired her. "We're going to try using people like these," he said, and Malia, her personality, her graciousness, her Hawaiianness—she had everything. She asked if she could sit in on the Culture Committee. Usually she would not be sitting in on professional conferences, but the answer was yes. Before I knew it, she was a regular member. She became very close to Mrs. Pukui.

All sorts of cases were being presented, one by one. Jack Haertig would pull out certain healing concepts, and all of us looked to Mrs. Pukui for Hawaiian healing practice.

Q: *And from this came bicultural healing practices?*

Masaru: With Mrs. Pukui's knowledge, everything started to change. We were now all trying to learn. I came away with one simple lesson when she said one day, "For every Hawaiian curse, there is a Hawaiian cure." We located many concepts which make sense to workers today. The popular *ho'oponopono* comes to mind. Before you know it, people like Lynette and Richard Paglinawan and others were looking into how to translate these concepts into English understanding. This became their goal. Every spare chance, they were going into culture. The energy was all there. They just moved. Whether they were at QLCC working or not, meant nothing because they were so dedicated. The rest became history—the series *Nānā I Ke Kumu*.

PERPETUATING HAWAIIAN CULTURE

Masaru: Mrs. Pukui made a determination that she was going to teach all she knows. Richard was selected to learn the Hawaiian legends that related to different areas: Nānākuli, Wai'anae, Mākaha Valley, Waipahu, Hō'ae'ae, Pearl Harbor, and so on.

We became living witnesses to how kahunas were developed in the ancient Hawaiian practice. Certain individuals in the village were picked from the time they were young to be the future kahuna. I'm sure if we could have taken Richard back to the old days, he would not have been a social worker. He would have been the kahuna for telling the legends.

FRICTION

Masaru: In the meantime, the (QLCC) trustees got all shook up. The conservative ones were saying, "The Trust might be jeopardized by having federal money coming in. Hey, we might lose our non-profit status. It's dangerous." We fought it. Pinky fought it. He convinced them that our federally funded projects were demonstration projects.

We could have followed the strict deed of trust, but the words "social work" weren't used in the deed of trust. We picked up the ball and ran. I'm sure Clorinda Lucas (by then trustee chair) had a lot to do with our actions. Social work's method and approaches fit all into helping kids and helping families. A state agency cannot do that. I've been in state and private agencies, so I can swear to that. The state agency is the worst. In the state government, I always have to fight the status quo. (Chuckles.)

Honpa Hongwanji Mission named Masaru a Living Treasure for his humanitarian work.

Q: *Let's talk about Clorinda Lucas. How did you experience Clorinda in all of this?*

She was a tremendous force—MSW, New York School of Social Work... Pinky's mother-in-law. (Chuckles.) I don't know how many social workers from Hawai'i got a master's in social work back then. She was no longer doing social work, but she was tremendously active in the community. She was on commissions, often as the chair. She was the lead trustee at QLCC, and she and Pinky were close. The fact they were mother-in-law and son-in-law was potentially awkward, but it never had any impact because Pinky's decisions were good decisions.

But she was only one vote. So Clorinda could have been overruled. But we managed. You know, with Pinky doing all the presentations of these programs...no problem.

When I became the executive, she opened up quite a bit to me as well, and we became close.

A CONFLICT OF CONSCIENCE

After twelve years at QLCC, seven as executive director, Masaru moved to state government in 1975. He served as deputy director of the Department of Social Services and Housing (DSSH) under Andrew Chang, also a social worker (see Chapter 7). With his background on the State Parole Board, Masaru was given responsibility for the State Corrections Division. When a public cry arose for the execution of "cop killers," he was under pressure to testify for a capital punishment bill in the legislature, a bill belatedly supported by Gov. George R. Ariyoshi.

Masaru: I'm the governor's appointee. He's decided he's going for a limited restoration of capital punishment for the killing of police officers, prison guards, and other law enforcement. For me, it's black and white. Killing is not right.

Previously the DSSH—Andy Chang, me, Pinky Thompson—always testified *against* it. But when Ariyoshi supported the bill, it became a very difficult time in our relationship. As a deputy, I didn't need to meet the governor, so my job was to convince Andy, who was in a very sensitive position. Andy agreed with me, and he helped me get the message over. I wrote what I believed, and this went direct to the governor. I'm deputy director in charge of public safety. If this law ever passes, I have to get funding to restore the hanging room in O'ahu Prison. No way you're getting me involved in that. Andy and I kept trying. "Governor, just stay neutral because this law may never pass." He replies, "Okay

Masaru Oshiro, a force for healing.

Andy, Masaru doesn't have to testify." Then when the hearing comes, the attorney general testifies for the administration, which is the role we were supposed to play.

Eventually, the Senate passes the bill and it goes over to the House. So I said, "This is where I stand." The governor calls me in and gives me permission to testify against the bill. I said there was something else to consider, which was the reaction of my colleagues. There are thirty-something deputy directors. They might think, "This guy's getting his great salary as a deputy director and he goes against the governor? How can he do this?" There is a hierarchy of loyalty. You're loyal to the governor. You don't argue with him. You get out.

The governor next asked if I wanted to transfer to another department. I said, "Same thing. I already have decided I will be testifying against the bill." Finally, the governor shakes my hand: "I'm really sorry to see you go." His staff writes a glowing press release about how great I am. (Chuckles.) And then in the last paragraph the governor says that it's good to know that somebody believes in something even if they have to give up a job. And best wishes in whatever I'd be doing.

With cuts in pay and status, Masaru took lower-level jobs in the state civil service. Between 1988 and 1991, he served as director of Alu Like, the private non-profit agency that Myron Thompson had founded. He was then appointed deputy director of the State Health Department for behavioral health, covering such crucial areas as drug abuse, alcoholism, and mental health. He retired in 1995 at the age of sixty-five. In retirement, he has devoted much of his time to the disaster relief work of the American Red Cross.

Masaru: I saw Red Cross as a way of getting back in direct touch with people who need help. I was deployed to an almost unimaginable list of air crashes, floods, hurricanes, and tornados at a rate of several a year. In October 2001, I was deployed by the Red Cross to the site of the World Trade Center disaster. The skills of social work, of empathy, and putting yourself in the other person's shoes are much in need in a disaster, and the work has been tremendously gratifying. It's social work pure and simple.

Q: *Your proudest moment in social work?*

Masaru: That's easy. It's when my daughter decided to become a social worker! ✦

CHAPTER 5

Lynette Paglinawan

Lynette Kaopuiki Paglinawan's mark in social work history is her singular contribution to the revived Hawaiian practice of ho'oponopono and, more broadly, to the Hawaiian cultural renaissance. Her personal story is seamless. It is about her integration of "self," by which she was enabled to perform her remarkable work. In this, she collaborated with her husband, Richard Paglinawan, like her a social worker of historic importance. Together they expanded the processes of resolving conflicts within, and empowering, the family. In a fusion of social work and Hawaiian cultural practice, their achievements have extended to institutions and whole communities.

A VIEW OF CHINATOWN

Lynette Paglinawan: When I was a small child our family lived with my grandparents in Pauoa Valley in Honolulu, which then was practically country. Then we moved to Chinatown, at the corner of Smith Street and Beretania. My father was a stevedore on the waterfront, only several blocks away. We lived in a flat on the second floor, which today would be called a tenement.

It was a real eye opener. We could look down when the police raided the bar across the street and see the fights and the prostitution. We'd see times when men were drunk, and arguments were going on between girlfriends and boyfriends high on drugs and getting into a beef, and more cops would be coming. On the Smith Street side, there was a community center for retired Chinese people to play *mah-jongg*, clouded with a lot of smoke.

I first saw all this with the eyes of a protected child. I was reared in a family that valued children, with close connections to our extended 'ohana. My parents were very conscious of protecting me and my sister. They were strict about *what* we could do, *when* we could do things, and *where* we could go by ourselves.

I learned survival skills early. Living across from a park, I began to realize I was well-coordinated and alert. The groups would often select me to be a team captain in volleyball, so I would pick members. It bothered me that the girls who were less agile got left behind. I could see the expressions on their faces. So when I got to make selections, I would pick three athletic players and then I went to the less agile. I placed a strong person with each of them to give support. Strategizing for me came naturally, because when you play in the park with the neighborhood kids, you don't just sit around. You've got to be on your toes. You've got to be alert. You've got to be thinking.

During the Depression when taro was hard to come by, I had to wake up early in the morning and stand in line to get my bag of poi, because the fish, the *'ōpae*, and the poi were always on our table. Besides my (brown) skin color, I have an Oriental look. The lady in the poi shop said, "Filipino girl, you don't belong over here. Go outside and wait." I stood up to her. I said, "I'm Hawaiian and I want my poi." And that dealt with it.

My mother was a custodian at my elementary school. I had a teacher who sent another student out during recess to bring me into the classroom. I said, "How come? What for?" A girl in our class had a seizure and made a mess of things, and the teacher told me to clean it up. I said, "That's not my job." The teacher was so upset, she called my mother in and said, "You have an impudent daughter." I didn't know what that word meant! My mother reported her to the principal, and she got reprimanded, and mother told me, "You did good."

Q: *What do you think the teacher was saying?*

Lynette: That I was somebody of a lower status. If your skin was darker, you're not part of the "preferred membership." It made me angry, so I came back with my answers. In hindsight, my parents armed me with, "This is life in the raw. You've got to know how to deal with it. But in our family, we don't treat people like that."

Lynette Paglinawan, surrounded here by her haumana *(students), is the foremost living perpetuator and teacher of* ho'oponopono.

You know what I noticed about myself? I learned very early if you keep your mouth shut, then nothing's going to change. So I learned to express what I wanted, and what I felt I needed, very early.

Q: *We should clarify for the reader: What is your ethnicity?*

Lynette: Hawaiian. My dad was pure Hawaiian. My mom was half Japanese. My grandmother was pure Japanese. My grandfather on my mother's side was half Hawaiian, half Caucasian. In the ninth grade, I went to Kamehameha Schools, where we were all Hawaiian, so identity or color at that point made very little difference.

I spent summers with my father's family on Moloka'i. When the Kū'ē (protest) petition against annexation was finally brought to light in 1998, I found the signatures of my family from Hālawa opposing it, and the signatures of my grandfather and his mama, opposing it with their signatures as well.

They were taro farmers in Hālawa, five generations on this land, in an isolated valley with no running water and no electricity. They had a poi factory, so they not only raised the taro but made the poi, and then they delivered it along the way to all the 'ohana and into Kaunakakai (town).

I loved going back there. I learned I am proud to be Hawaiian, and I am proud to bear the color. It's who we are and what we do that earns us the right to be proud. So I didn't see Honolulu being my only *hānau* (birthplace). My *hānau* is in Hālawa on Moloka'i.

Q: *Did you grow up speaking Hawaiian?*

Lynette: No.

Q: *Not at all?*

Lynette: Not at all. My parents said to me, "If you're going to make it in life, you have to speak English.[22] My mother, having worked in an educational setting, concluded that education was the pathway to get ahead. I grew up being encouraged, "Do your homework." She couldn't help me much, so I had to do homework on my own. I wanted to get an education. I wanted to succeed. I wanted to experience differences. I wanted to be able to travel, to see different environments, and how other people lived.

Lynette graduated from Kamehameha Schools in 1957. She was the first of her family to attend college, enrolling at Bradley University in Peoria, Illinois.

Lynette: I felt pretty sure of myself, but it doesn't mean I wasn't scared. I was shaking on the plane, and getting off and looking at a sea of white faces.

---

22   Eventually Lynette took Hawaiian language classes at UH from Samuel Elbert, co-author with Mary Kawena Pukui of *The Hawaiian-English Dictionary*.

Q: *All white people looked alike!*

Lynette: (Laughs.) Yeah! Anyway, it was exciting but scary. Most people were nice. But I also got to see racism. When we got on the bus, black people automatically had to go the back. The conductor didn't know where I belonged, so I would go to the back because some of my friends were Negroes. That didn't bother me. My roommate came from Korea. She looked fully Oriental. That didn't bother us. We sat where our friends were. If we didn't have a Negro person with us, we'd look wherever the window was available and we'd sit to be comfortable.

Many of the members of the Bradley basketball team were Negroes. When they went into the bar, there was a side for the Negroes and they could not go into the other side. I'd say to myself, "How can this be happening in America?"

My father often had talked about doing things in a very Hawaiian way. Being away from home, I began to see what "a very Hawaiian way" meant. It meant don't wait until people ask you for something. You're supposed to be alert to their needs. Before someone asks, you help. When I was invited to my friend's home for Christmas vacation, I saw her mother doing the laundry and the ironing and then getting the food ready. I was being treated as a guest, but I felt badly to have my seniors waiting on me. Meanwhile, my classmate was sitting down. I couldn't believe that. I told her I was going into the kitchen to talk story with her mother. My motive was to make myself useful. I didn't wait for her to ask. In return she wanted to do something special for me. She cooked fish, *freshwater* fish, and I forced myself to eat it, even if it tasted so muddy.

Q: *Catfish!*

Lynette: Yes! In the Hawaiian culture, you don't criticize what people offer you. You take it and you eat it. So my training at home kept me in good stead. At the end of the week, the woman embraced me and said she wished she had a daughter like me.

Q: *You were there in the late 1950s. Did you have any sense there was something in the air with regard to race relations?*

Lynette: Many people were nice. In fact, being from Hawai'i was a "wow." But there was a beginning of anger. I myself would make statements like, "This should not be." But that was the extent to which I would venture anything. I realized what you espouse is one thing, but making it happen is another. If the ideal is honorable and the intention is good, how do you bring about change?

Q: *When did social work become your conscious goal?*

Lynette: It was that ninth-grade year at Kamehameha. The teacher asked us to write about a career idea. What would we like to be when we grew up? I thought and I thought, and I wrote that I wanted to be a social worker. The name Clorinda Lucas came up. She was the one Hawaiian I found listed as a social worker, and she became a model.

After two years at Bradley, I returned to Hawai'i because it was difficult for my parents to afford two children going to the university. I had been away and I knew what worked for me was to reconnect with people. I sought out other graduates from Kamehameha. I found the sisters in the sorority Ke Ānuenue, and they invited me in. I balanced fun and socializing with getting the grades during two years of UH "undergrad" so I could enter graduate school.

FINDING HAWAIIAN CULTURE IN SOCIAL WORK

Lynette met and married Richard Paglinawan, then the only Native Hawaiian in the School of Social Work. On Richard's graduation, Lynette enrolled, again becoming, as she remembered it, the only Native Hawaiian in the school.

Lynette: It was lonely. (Chuckles.) When we talk about Hawaiian culture in the School of Social Work, it wasn't on the table. It never crossed my mind. Richard, meanwhile, worked at Salvation Army Boy's Home and then he followed Pinky [Thompson] over to Queen Lili'uokalani

Children's Center.

Richard was working with a boy who was obsessed with an early death. The boy's mother told him he was cursed. When Richard heard the word "cursed," he said, "Social work never taught me how to handle this." He went to Masaru Oshiro and Masaru asked what he wanted to do. Richard said, "I want to talk to my tūtū." And that's how Mary Kawena Pukui came to help QLCC. Richard had studied archaeology, and in the process he had become acquainted with her at Bishop Museum, and from that time on she was the main cultural source, every week, of what became the QLCC Culture Committee.

Richard often talked about how amazing it was that as he encountered things in his life's journey, something opened for him. In graduate school, he had firsthand experience with ghostly encounters, so many things were letting him know, "You're a Hawaiian. These things happen but you folks don't know the reason why. You have to go outside to see a kahuna who can tell you what this is about." It was crucial that Richard knew how to approach Tūtū Pukui, because many of the staff on the Culture Committee were very Western in their approach. Often she couldn't quite understand what they wanted, so Richard would have to ask their questions from Hawaiian experience, and then Tūtū could respond.

Q: *Richard was mixed Hawaiian and Filipino.*

Lynette: Yes. His father was Filipino. Dad was very quiet. He went to work. He brought the money home to feed the family. His mama (Richard's grandmother) and all his younger siblings went back to the Philippines to live. When Richard and I got married, his family thought all the Hawaiian things we did were Filipino in origin. I looked at Richard and I said, "They don't know this as Hawaiian, yeah?" And he said, "No." (Chuckles.) From my perspective, the Filipino influence was not that strong. Mom did become a Catholic because Dad was a Catholic, but she was the dominant one in the family. She took care of everything.

Q: *So, what were you learning as a beginning social worker?*

Lynette: My practicum placements included a stint at the Department of Health and Disabilities Unit, and we got cases there in the first year. On day one in my second year of practicum [with the Salvation Army's Children's Facilities Mānoa Unit], I had a caseload of students who lived in the cottages. So I wasn't afraid of being assigned a caseload. I really wanted to develop my clinical skills—and I was always open to looking at myself and looking at my influence on the clients. The track I was on was to know myself in fuller, deeper ways. This is an important part of being a good social worker. I fully agree with the idea that you have to begin with yourself. You have to know yourself.

When I graduated, I went to work at QLCC, like Richard. All this time I had thought about Clorinda Lucas, and now I learned she was a trustee of QLCC. I was happy to be there. I was a sponge. I was an eager beaver for culture consultation. I realized that while I was raised in a home that was basically Hawaiian, it was *haole* at the same time. When I'm with the family, then my Hawaiian side was emphasized. If I was in a non-Hawaiian situation, I also knew how to handle myself. Kamehameha Schools taught me that. But it was almost as if I had a Hawaiian side and a Western side.

Doing intakes with Hawaiian families, I recognized early they were describing things for which they did not have labels. I could pick it up immediately. I could recognize a situation even if I didn't know how to handle it. And so I asked their permission. I would say, "I don't know about this, but I know it is Hawaiian. Can I go ask somebody for help?" When they said yes, I would take it to Culture Committee.

With the opportunity to do psychiatric consultation and then to participate in cultural consultation, my two sides began to merge. I recognized I'm not just *here* and I'm not just *there*, but I'm centered in this one body. Uniting the parts. What you know up *here* (touches head) and what you felt down *here* (stomach) are now all together.

That was a wonderful time. I think by three years after I graduated, my skills as a practitioner were good. It was a golden time of discovery and exploration and solidification. It's me, it's all of me. (Chuckles.) And I liked it.

The progress of transformation became obvious for the managers and the administrative staff within a short period of time. After I took a leave to give birth to our third child in 1969, I was asked if I would be interested in doing a research project to demonstrate the usefulness and viability of *ho'oponopono.* Of course, I said yes.

Q: *What should we focus on in terms of* ho'oponopono? *It's a big, complicated subject.*

Lynette: Let's begin at the beginning. Richard and I, we were very different. Richard was born to the mold. I had to acquire it (laughter). Richard is a thinker. He had intended to go into the priesthood. As a boy, he was very active in the

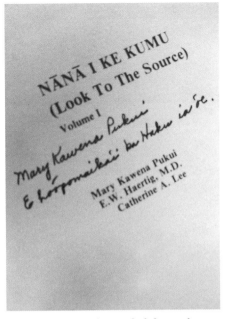

Lynette's work descended from the venerable Mary Kawena Pukui, the primary consultant for QLCC's Nānā I Ke Kumu (Look to the Source) *project.*

Catholic church—an altar boy and all of that. For one of his classes in religion, there was a debate. "Does God exist?" He wanted to be on the pro-Christian side, but he got selected to be on the negative side. He won the debate. The teacher commended him for his depth of research. This debate question had profound implications beyond what the students would have been able to deal with. This was in the ninth grade, and he decided he's not going into the priesthood.

So that's Richard. Anything he gets involved in, he's going to do with gusto to reach that deeper level. Growing up, he was under the influence of his (Hawaiian) grandfather. He's more familiar with spirits than I was at that age. I only heard it secondhand, but it was very much a part of him.

He is very likeable, very even-tempered, thoughtful and polite. He didn't struggle with the inner questions of identity as I did.

When I learned how much the *ho'oponopono* project was going to impact the lives of clients, I got scared. I realized it was not just about working with culture and cultural activities. There was a heavy *kuleana* (responsibility) behind this, a *kuleana* for my cultural heritage and for clients.

We had a technical advisory team with members from the program staff, the university, the Department of Social Services, and the broader community. When I expressed my hesitations, they tried to support me, in essence saying, "It's good you brought it up. It's what people go through when they start a challenging journey." That was, to me, a haole response, but I was worried about the Hawaiian side. I was a student of hula under 'Iolani Luahine (a legendary teacher and dancer). She taught me that certain Hawaiian traditions are reserved for certain individuals. I went to see Tūtū Pukui, and I expressed my dilemma to her. I asked if I had an inheritance sanction to do this work, based on the past. I said I couldn't track the genealogy, and she gave me the genealogy. Lo and behold, on the paternal side of the family, we had healers. Armed with that, I felt okay.

Q: *What a story!*

Lynette: There's more. One day my aunt came to family dinner and said to me, "This is too dangerous. Don't do *ho'oponopono*. You don't know what's going to happen. You don't know what's going to happen to your family." We had an old circular library table that could seat fifteen people in this very room. My mother was there, and her posture changed immediately. Her eyes seemed to be looking into my soul. She had a possession experience, a *noho* experience. The voice that came through her was not her voice. It didn't sound like her. At first, I thought it might be my grandfather. But it wasn't his voice. The only thing that came out of her mouth was, "The silent stranger is leaving. Your way is clear."

Through consultation, Mrs. Pukui and Dr. Haertig concluded that the voice of the spirit that spoke to Lynette was that of her maternal grandfa-

Lynette with the moai *stones of Rapa Nui, off the coast of South America. Through authentic cultural revival, Lynette and her husband, Richard Likeke Paglinawan, touched people not only in Hawai'i but throughout the Pacific.*

ther's 'aumakua, *or lineal family god, whose identity he had never shared with Lynette's mother.*

Lynette: Tūtū said, "Your '*aumakua* has sanctioned you to do this."[23] As a result I shed all my fears and I entered *ho'oponopono* with an attitude that no one can stop me. If I didn't know something, I had my elders. I had resources to turn to. The intentions were good, and with that I could go forward. Fascinating. I felt whole.

---

23 Lynette defined '*aumakua* as "an ancestor who, in his or her lifetime, did extraordinary things and stood out in the family, especially in the realm of spirituality. These were considered special gifts from higher powers. At the point they died, they may not be known as 'aumakua. But their stories are passed to the descendants in the way stories of my grandfather have been passed down to my generation and we're passing it down to our children. So it becomes an idealized person as when we put my grandfather on the pedestal. We remember the outstanding, the phenomenal things that they were able to do. By retaining stories, we foster a connection to a member of my ancestry I've never known. I may not know his name. I just know that the spiritual entity from within our family line has been a source of help for my grandfather, and if he's been a source of help for my grandfather, I can presume that it's not just for him but for all of our family."

In 1972, Hui Hanai, the auxiliary support group of QLCC, published the classic work Nānā I Ke Kumu, *which defined* hoʻoponopono *as "setting to right; to make right…to restore and maintain good relationships…[a] family conference in which relationships were 'set right' through prayer, discussion, confession, repentance, and mutual restitution and forgiveness."[24] Ten pages of discussion followed.*

Lynette: The gift of *hoʻoponopono* is that it allows us a process to talk it out. Once we forgive, we can take on responsibility and follow through with it. You have to have love for yourself and for others. If you have love, then you live in a way that puts you in balance with the higher powers you believe in, and the aloha spirit can come through and you can be generous and kind.

Q: *When I came to Hawaiʻi fifty years ago, Hawaiian spiritual practices—kahuna ʻanāʻana—had a consistently scary or negative connotation. If people knew anything about kahuna tradition, it was thought of as a dark art.*

Lynette: Duality.

Q: *Duality?*

Lynette: Hawaiians lived in a system of duality. In our training and in the readings I've done, healers have said, "You need to know the black magic in order to be able to counter it. So you have the potential to use it negatively as well as positively." Duality relates to what Richard and I talk about: the Kū (fierce male god) and the Hina (nurturing female deity). Opposites. The Kū and the Hina are a part of the makeup of each person. So there's a potential for the femininity as well as the masculinity—the aggression, the hostility—all within an appropriate context. You need to know what you're dealing with.

---

24   *Nānā I Ke Kumu* (I), 60

Following in Pinky Thompson's footsteps, Richard Paglinawan moved from QLCC to leadership positions in the government of the State of Hawai'i. He served as deputy director of the Department of Hawaiian Homes, then as deputy director of the Department of Social Services and Housing. He also served as chief administrative officer of the Office of Hawaiian Affairs and then was recruited by the legendary political organizer, Robert C. Oshiro, to be the cultural consultant of Queen Emma Foundation.

Meanwhile, Lynette took the lead in the renewed practice of ho'opono-pono. *By this time, the process of Hawaiian cultural renewal was in full sway. Widely dispersed elements of the community were suddenly ready to try out what Lynette and Richard had retrieved with the guidance of Mrs. Pukui. They acted as trainers and guides and also as creators and keepers of standards. Drawing on Richard's training in group work, they adapted ho'oponopono to address the needs of large families, social programs, and even whole communities. Through collaboration with the Native Hawaiian Bar Association, the practice of ho'oponopono was integrated into the court system and the prison system. Their work also extended to the School of Social Work, Family Court, the UH medical school, Alu Like, the Hawaiian Learning Program, Legal Aid, and others.*

In 1990, Lynette became the executive director of Bishop Museum's Native Hawaiian Culture and the Arts program. In Richard's continued hands-on cultural work, he, along with Lynette and several other collaborators, revived the Hawaiian practice of lua, *the rituals and training of the* kanaka maoli *warrior. He passed away in 2018 at the age of 78. As of this writing, Lynette is kupuna-in-residence at the University of Hawai'i at West O'ahu. She teaches ho'oponopono in its Hawaiian and Indigenous Health concentration. Among Lynette and Richard's many honors, each was named a Living Treasure by the Honpa Hongwanji Mission of Hawai'i.* ✦

CHAPTER 6

Patti Lyons

The social justice story of Patti Lyons began in a small town in Indiana. Born in 1937, she was mostly raised by a grandmother who gave her both love and the power of listening. She migrated to Hawai'i in 1965 with a social work degree in hand. She volunteered to leave the security of client work in downtown Honolulu for the uncertainties of a poverty-stricken rural community.

There she saw through the veil of child abuse. Government agencies, including social workers, had looked the other way. Patti saw and acted, with indignation, courage, and compassion. She was treated as a pariah, but she persisted.

GROWING UP

Patti Lyons: We were very poor. My mother was too young when she gave birth to take care of me, so I lived with my grandmother from the time I was—I don't even know. I don't think I was walking.

My grandmother sacrificed. She carried big buckets of coal and baked angel food cakes that she sold for two dollars. She was a switchboard operator for the county, and people respected her. Probably because she listened in to some of their calls, and she knew everything that was going on.

In the county there were about two thousand people. She knew them all. She knew all their phone numbers. She'd have to get up at night and answer emergency calls if somebody got sick. She was an outstanding role model in terms of truthfulness, transparency, and honesty. She had it all for me—her values.

We had a small screened-in back porch. One day she told me, "I want you to stay right here." She went outside into the cold and got a Black man and brought him in to the back porch. I remember he had a little knapsack on his back. She said to me, "Don't you ever say a word about this." I guess I said, "I won't, Grandma. I won't say anything." But I didn't know about what.

He looked like he wasn't gonna make it, but she got him settled with some blankets and something hot to drink and some food. Then she told me, "The rule of this town is that darkies cannot be here after sunset"—she called them darkies. "So you must never say anything." I wasn't up the next morning early enough, but she gave him food for his knapsack and sent him on his way as the sun was rising—so he would not be harmed. I remember it vividly, and I never said anything for years and years, and then I wrote it in a paper.

Q: *Was she religious?*

Patti: Yes. She didn't go to church all the time because she had to work a lot on Sundays, but she always sent me. It was a Disciples of Christ church, something like that. I know we believed in love and forgiveness and compassion. That's always been a big part of my life.

Q: *You identify with those who are suffering. Are you an escapee from suffering?*

Patti: Maybe there was a feeling of abandonment. I felt my parents growing apart and I probably suffered some from that. I always felt a little bit abandoned by my mother because she was too young. She couldn't take care of me. She didn't really know how or what or why. My grandmother came a long way on a bus to where my mother and father were living in this little town. I held up my arms like this. (Motions)

That's really making me sad. Sorry. It was, "Take me. Take me."

She told my mother, "Let me just take her for a while. You're having your hands full. Let me take her for a while." I remember going back on the bus, as little as I was, being in my grandmother's arms.

Her house was tiny, one room and a tiny little kitchen with a hand pump for water. Then you went up some steps and that was the switchboard room with a bed where my grandmother would sleep at night. We had a teensy little yard with telephone poles in it. I've always thought it had creosote on the telephone poles, and maybe that has caused some of my cancers—I don't know. Anyway, I would play on it with bare feet. I'm dating this back to the 1940s, because one day when I was outside playing, I went into the house to get a drink of water and there was my grandfather with tears rolling down his face and my grandmother, with her head in her hands, sobbing. I thought, "What is this? Are they gonna' die?" because my father had just been killed in a motorcycle accident and I had seen him in a coffin. I must have been six years old. I said, "Grandma, Grandma, what's wrong?" She said, "Patti, the president (Franklin Roosevelt) died." They were poor, and they were Republicans, and I couldn't understand why they were both crying. She said, "Patti, he was a good man.'"

Q: *What about your schooling?*

Patti: My grandmother always said, "You're the only one that has ever gone to school." She only went to the eighth grade. Smart, but she only went to eighth grade, and my mother had dropped out at sixteen. Grandmother said, "It'd be so good if you could be a teacher." So she sent me to a girls school where I wanted to go in Missouri, William Woods College, and I got an associate degree. Then I went on to Butler University in Indianapolis, and I got my undergraduate degree. Then I taught for two years in a high school. English and Speech. They were kids who really needed help.

One kid—she was so skinny and scrawny, this girl, but so smart. She could never give a book report. She would start laughing hysterically. And then the class would start laughing and eventually I would start laughing, but I had said, "If you don't give a book report you're going to get an 'F' and you won't pass the class."

She came in one day and said, "I'm sorry I can't give the book report. I really want to." She started to cry. She told me how her mother would take a broom handle to her and go like this (motions), and she would hide under the bed. I gave her the lead in a school play. All the other teachers said, "Oh, you can't do that, she's gonna mess everything up. She's gonna start giggling and you're selling tickets to this play for the community. You're absolutely crazy to do that." But she did a beautiful job.

A DOORWAY TO SOCIAL WORK

Patti: I worked for the Indiana State Department of Public Welfare during the summers of the two years I taught. They said, "We'll give you a stipend if you will agree that you'll go back and get a master's in social work and then you'll come to work for us. You have to commit for two years after you get your master's, but we'll pay you well." I decided since I could never really help these kids the way it was, that's what I would do.

I got my master's at the university in 1961. Each of my two years there I got into trouble over advocacy. The first year, they didn't call my name for a field work assignment, so I had to hold up my hand at the end and say, "My name wasn't called." I had just prayed, "Give me anything, anything whatsoever, except medical." The instructor said, "OK, I'm sorry I didn't call your name. We're going to assign you to the Indiana University Medical Center and you're going to work at the children's hospital."

My first case was a cancer patient, a woman who was going to die. She had five children. When I went into her room, she said, "I don't want you in here. I don't want anybody in here because nobody really cares about me." I asked, "Why do you say that?" She said, "This young doctor came in today and I told him, 'You can't put anything in my veins anymore. They're collapsed. There's nothing. Why do it? I'm going to die.'"

She accused the doctor of not caring. He shot back, "You're right, I don't." I tried to reassure the woman, "I'm sure he didn't mean that." I thought maybe she had misunderstood. He came in while I was there and he said, "I'm sorry about what I said to you this morning." And at that point, I said, "This guy should not be in medicine."

I went to my supervisor and told her about it. I said, "You've got to get him out of medicine." This was a hospital for teaching doctors, so she was horrified. She said, "Well, I'll talk with [the director], but I don't know that he will be kicked out. How about if I give you some Compazine?" she said to me—you know, the tranquilizer.

Q: *Meaning, "Why don't we tranquilize you instead?"*

Patti: Yes. Why don't we tranquilize you? Let's treat you rather than treat the doctor.

It was a time when social workers were supposed to be entirely objective. They thought I had too much emotion, too much subjectivity, that I got too involved with my clients. So, actually, I took the Compazine, because I felt so identified with that kid and with his mother that I said, "Well, maybe I'm not objective. Maybe I am too emotionally involved."

The second year of practicum, the dean of social work used to talk about how families should be allowed to have contraception: Women should be told about birth control so they don't have so many children. Well, my second placement was at an adoption agency where the two top executives were both Catholic. I had a case where the woman really needed Planned Parenthood, and wanted it, and they wouldn't allow me to refer her, so I went to the dean. I said the girl really needs contraception and that she would use it. The agency gave me the grade, so it's a wonder they let me graduate.

Some of my professors I really liked and enjoyed and got something out of, but I didn't feel that the values of social work at that time, at least for me, really helped people. They talked a good game, but what did they really do for people?

Q: *In social work classes, did they ever talk about relationship formation and listening and accepting people at face value?*

Patti: They talked about it, and it was in the books. There was a lot of theory about it, but I just didn't see it in action. I think I learned about listening from my grandmother.

Q: *Possibly you were propelled by the difference between theory and what you saw in reality?*

Patti: Mm-hmm (affirmative). Immediately after graduation, I started working for the Indiana State Department of Public Welfare. I had thirteen counties around Indianapolis. I was able to talk to people and find out how they were hurting, and what policies needed to be changed because

Patti Lyons first became widely known in Hawai'i for exposing and criminalizing child abuse.

they were punitive. They were somewhat different in the different counties, because culture was sometimes different in this county from that county. Child welfare services were really nonexistent, so I helped establish a child welfare service.

In the process, I learned about collaboration of the courts and the police and the welfare department and the public health nurses. They were all interested in helping. I didn't find anybody who was not. Most people were interested in trying to form a system that would work for children and families.

In 1964, they took me off my job to do a federal review of welfare. All we were to do is observe. For example, we were supposed to ask, "Was there a man in the house that wasn't supposed to be?" I was always told that the women were having children to get more money from welfare. I went to an area in Indianapolis, almost all Black, and I went into one home where the mother had several children. They had a pot-bellied stove. I previously had a little seven-year-old—I remember his name, Bobby—who had been horribly burned by a stove like that. I still remember his screams. I looked at the little kids and realized they might touch the stove because winters were terribly cold and the stove was red hot.

Remember, I was supposed to be doing a "review," and reviewers weren't supposed to do anything for the families. I went back to where I lived, which was about thirty miles away, and got blankets for them and also some canned food, hoping I could help them at least temporarily.

HAWAI'I

Patti: While getting started in social work, I got married. My husband, Andy, had gone back to school because he was a parole officer, and he wanted to work inside a prison where he could do group work. When he finished, he made applications and got job offers in Alaska and Hawai'i. That was in late 1965, and we decided to move to Hawai'i, just a few years after statehood.

At this same time, I was facing my first bout with cancer. I remember my mother telling me, "It's so wonderful. You're not going to have radiation—they would have told you by now—because everybody that has radiation that we know of has died." I said, "Yeah, that's really great." She walked out of the room, and the doctor walked in. He said, "By the way, we're going to start your radiation treatments this next week." I thought I was going to die. Afterward in Hawai'i, I stayed home a whole year, because it was unknown after the radiation what would happen to me. I was badly burned.

We lived in Hale'iwa on the North Shore of O'ahu and Andy worked at the Oahu Community Correctional Center. He did his group work and apparently was really successful at it. The prisoners liked him. He made life better for a lot of them. He was a good listener. I met many of them—in fact a couple guys stayed at our house. One's name was Carl, a pretty affable guy. I liked him. He had done some big crime, a robbery or something. I always try to see the good in people. There is both good and bad, but let's try to see what's good. Carl had paid his price.

In early 1967 I was recovered enough to look for a job, and I went to Child and Family Service. The director said, "We could hire you as the highest level of social worker, which would be a social worker four. You would see mainly middle income and upper income military officers and their wives and you would do therapy with them."

I said, "Don't you have anything else?" She was kind of shocked and she said, "Well we have this place way out on the Wai'anae Coast and they need a social worker." She said nobody would want to work out there. Child and Family had never had an outreach office—people came in to get counseling—and I said, "Why is that?" Her answer was, "First of all, it's a very low-income community. There are no transportation services, no medical, no dental, no welfare office, and they are mainly Hawaiians and they don't like haoles."

The director said she would let me go to Wai'anae one day a week. My office was to be in the Wai'anae Church in the Sunday school room. "Don't assume it's going to last," she said, "because you're not going to have any clients. They're not going to come see you."

Q: *Why do you think Wai'anae was so badly off?*

Patti: There was poverty. If you wanted to look at poverty and deprivation, that certainly existed. At the time alcohol was more prevalent than drugs. Maybe a lack of success. Maybe a lack of ambition caused by poverty. Everybody has tried to do something about poverty.

Q: *And who do you recall being there to help?*

Patti: The church secretary, the school nurse, the public health people—we got together and asked, "What are we lacking out here the most?" We asked clients, "What do you think? What's most needed?"

I visited the schools. They knew I was there, and they would come to see me after school. One of the women had a husband who drank heavily and abused her. I helped her get a restraining order. One day she called and said, "Come up, please come up quickly." She sounded like she'd been crying and the kids were crying. Her nose was red—you could tell she had been bleeding—and the curtains were burning. Her husband had set fire to the curtains. He was walking around and he was pretty drunk. She asked me what to do, so I called Sergeant Carlos to come down. I pointed out the restraining order and the curtains burning, her nose and everything. But Sergeant Carlos said, "I can't do anything because I didn't see him hit her."

I said, "So this restraining order that we worked so hard to get means nothing?" The sergeant said, "Not unless I see him hit her." About that time the husband comes up and he goes like this (swings) at Sergeant Carlos and Sergeant Carlos arrested him for hitting a police officer. The husband was taken down to the jail. I was helping her get her stuff packed and a place for her and her kids to go. Then the phone rings and it's the husband and he says, "Hello, Miss Lyons." I said, "Yes?" He said, "My bail is twenty-five dollars. Do you think you could bring it down?" I said, "No I can't. You have to stay in there for a while."

In three months, I had a waiting list of families who wanted to see me. I had kids who needed dental care badly and I had volunteers who took them to Strong-Carter Dental Clinic in Pālama. When they needed, I would take kids to Family Court, because the parents worked in the pineapple fields and couldn't go with them.

When I went back to the Child and Family office, I said, "Hey, I do have clients and I think I ought to be out there more." So then the director sent me two days a week and finally full time.

CHILD ABUSE

Q: *Let's go from the ground up. Who was there with their problems and what kind of problems were they having?*

Patti: The image along the Wai'anae Coast was about happy kids and parents who took care of them and loved their children. (Patti pauses to share photos of a battered child). There were abused children as well.

Q: *Did you take those photos?*

Patti: The police took them. That was a time when they gave photos out to me as a social worker. You know? Those were cigarette burns.

Q: *My God.*

Patti: Scaldings (shares more photos).

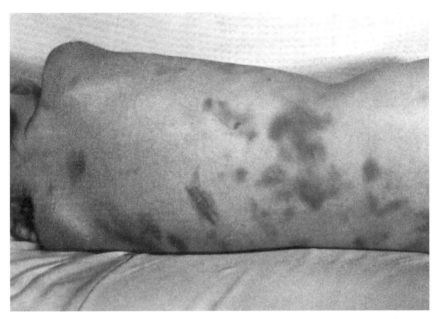

Publication of victims' photographs helped open the subject of child abuse for public discussion.

Q: *Oh, God—how was it that of all the things you faced, child abuse rose to the top?*

Patti: In Indiana as well as Hawai'i, services for abused children were being ignored. Parents needed help with how to relate to their children. Some of them could accept that help. Some couldn't. I saw so much suffering from it. I saw different types of it regularly.

I had incest situations. I don't know how they all got referred to me, but I had the gambit. A girl twelve years old having a baby by her father.

One girl I remember so well. She told me her stomach was hurting. She said her father had hit her in the stomach really hard. She said this wasn't the first time—that she had been hospitalized before, and I said, "Really?" That's before you believed everything that a child said. I asked who the doctor was. I called him and told him she was in my office and her stomach was really hurting.

The doctor said, "Maybe she is having internal bleeding."

I said, "Don't you want to examine her? Aren't you going to do something about it?"

He said, "No, I've reported this case many times, and DHS doesn't do anything. I've gotten in trouble with the family for it, and now I'm finished with it."

I called Sergeant Carlos again, and he said to bring her down to the police station. When we got there, he told me, "Now you whisper in her ear and you tell her to run outside and then I'm going to go outside and arrest her." I said, "But she is the victim, not the perpetrator."

"Look," he said, "do you want her to get medical help or not?" and I said I did. He said, "Well, then she has got to go down to the Juvenile Detention Home. I'm going to put down PINS—person in need of supervision. She'll go down to the detention home and she'll get medical help."

We formed a little committee for the protection of children in Wai'anae—we sat around the kitchen table. We went to the DHS office to try to convince them they weren't doing anything about the cases we sent them. They said, "Well, your philosophy is different from ours." I said, "What is that?" They said, "We believe that children belong with their natural parents." (I was constantly being told, "Children belong with their parents.") I said, "I believe that children belong with their natural parents unless they are going to die or be harmed for life," and it ended like that. As we walked out the door, I said, "I'm going to go higher." When we got out the door I said to the minister, "What does 'higher' mean?" because I had no idea. It turned out we decided to take the issue of child abuse to the legislature.

Q: *Who was "we"?*

Patti: We had a school nurse, a public health nurse, a secretary from Nānākuli School, and somebody from the Community Action Program. We also had somebody from Legal Aid. Altogether we had about a dozen people, and all of us had child abuse cases—lots of cases.

One case involved a thirteen-year-old girl who ran away from home and said the reason was that her stepfather had forced her to have sexual relations with him and that the stepfather was always running his hands over her body. The social worker who investigated the case told the legislators that the stepfather confessed having had sexual relations with the girl, and then the mother said, "He was just checking her out."

One legislator who heard us was Dickie (Richard H.S.) Wong. In the hearing he said to DHS, "So I understand that children get sent to a detention home when they have been abused?" They said, "No." He turned to me and he said, "Patti, is that true?" I said, "It's true. I've got the police reports right here."

The DHS directors were angry. You could see it on their faces. They took a newspaper reporter out in the hallway and said that I and the other advocates were going to cause more child abuse because people would be afraid to report it.

DHS wrote to the board complaining about my work. It said essentially, "If you don't get rid of Ms. Lyons, and also my supervisor at Child and Family Service who supported me in all of this, I'm going to tell my workers not to give to Aloha United Way," which for us meant financial support. The chairman of our board, an attorney, took the letter and marched over to the DHS director's office. He walked right past the secretary and threw the letter down and said, "We may not always agree with what our staff does, but we won't ever muzzle them," and he walked out. The social workers at DHS and the top management signed a petition against me. They said I had been unprofessional and unethical in my behavior and that I should be kicked out of the National Association of Social Workers. They wrote me they were going to do an investigation, and I said, "Fine, do whatever you want to do, but I'm not coming to it." Then after they had done it they said, "We have exonerated you from all wrongdoing, and you are not unethical and unprofessional."

Thereafter the NASW in Hawai'i voted me the first Social Worker of the Year and gave me a check for a hundred dollars.

If you work long enough, things do change, because they did. We got child abuse defined in the law and we got a Child Protective Service Center established. Sixty-nine kids had been reported that first year statewide, and the following year there were over a thousand because of the publicity.

Q: *Was that the transitional year, Patti?*

Patti: I think it was 1969.

Q: *As context, how aware were you of the War on Poverty, as it was called?*

Patti: I was. I was in the Model Cities program (successor to the Community Action Program). Billions of dollars were spent on the War on Poverty and I didn't see many good outcomes, not as a result right then. Now, years later, I'm thrilled that the Waiʻanae Comprehensive Health is out there. I'm thrilled they have Hawaiian healers along with Western medical services. In fact, I was on the first Waiʻanae Comprehensive Health Center Board. I was the only person who lived outside the community and the only haole.

Who knows? Maybe the War on Poverty is what it took to get some things that were lasting.

Altogether I worked in Waiʻanae for seven years. After that, I was assigned back downtown and I became the director of Child and Family Service.

Q: *And this is where your life took another big turn.*

Patti: It was through our adoption program. The quality of service and the kids placed internationally were going down, down, down. I was worried about it. People were sending kids back. A family would take a child and then say, "This is not the kind of kid I wanted." They'll put him on a plane and send him back.

The numbers from the Philippines began to go down after [Ferdinand] Marcos was driven out and Corey Aquino was elected. I said to the adoption supervisor, "Maybe we had better go and find out why. Do they not like our program? Are we doing something wrong? What's happening?"

Officials in the Philippines said to me, "Why don't you help us keep

our children here in our own country."
When I went back to Hawai'i I told our
board chairman, Jeffrey [Watanabe],
"We have to do something."[24] I must have
been menopausal because I was crying
when I said that. Jeffrey agreed. He said
the Filipinos are the largest rising immigrant group, and we need to do something to help them. I said, "But Jeffrey,
we have to have some money." He said,
"Yes, and I'll tell you what, I will convince the board of directors of Child and
Family Service to give $50,000 for you
to go find the money." The board gave
me, of their own private money, $50,000
for me to see what I could do. I thought,
"Oh boy, piece of cake." I've always
found money. Some board members
resigned—there were at least two, maybe
three, who didn't agree with going to the
Philippines, and didn't agree with trying to raise money for it.

Patti opens a center for treatment of abuse with Myron Thompson, then director of the State Human Services Department.

We just accepted that's what happens. Jeffrey was okay with it, and I was okay with it.

Q: *The board members took the money out of their own pockets?*

Patti: Yeah...they made a donation.

Q: *That's a good board.*

Patti: It *was* a good board. They really supported me. To this day, the

---

24 Jeffrey Watanabe, a prominent Honolulu attorney, played a major role in these events, first as chairman of Child and Family Service, then as chairman of the Consuelo Foundation.

board is very generous—we have one hundred percent personal giving.

Then I began making all those fundraising talks...I made it to anybody who would listen. I went back to the Philippines repeatedly looking for a demonstration program. I settled on Baguio and the surrounding areas. That's where the government said that services were most needed, because it's a beautiful resort area and the foreign pedophiles were coming in.

Rose Cruz Churma—Rose is Filipina—wanted to adopt a child from the Philippines, and her phone call got put through to me—by mistake—instead of to the adoption staff. When she said something about being from Baguio I said, "Maybe we ought to talk." We spent an hour on the phone. She said, "I'll take you."

We took a bus from Manila up the island of Luzon. A very long trip. Our bus broke down in Tarlac, and we were out there for a long time with our baggage, luggage and everything. Finally we got to Baguio, and we found our demonstration project through an innovative guy— Danny Ucriccio—he was working with street kids who needed a shelter. He had a place in mind, but I still had no money to do it. Finally, I had to tell Danny I had failed. The tears were flowing.

And then I got a call from my secretary. "You'd better get back here soon. The staff are in a mutiny. They say that your place is in Hawai'i, not in the Philippines, and you better get back here. Because they're going to go to the board of directors and you have a chance of being fired." This is my secretary telling me that.

I said, "Just tell them I'm coming back tomorrow, and all of this is over with. I haven't found any money, so they can relax." Then at the end of the conversation, she said, "Oh, somebody wants to talk with you, something about a shelter for street children." I said, "Oh, just leave the number on my desk." I get back and that name Consuelo Alger was on my desk. That's the beginning, because she invited me to her house.

Q: *She reached out to you.*

Patti: Yes. She'd heard about what I was trying to do. She said, "I usually don't invite people to my house because they always end up asking me for money." When I walked in there's twenty-five people who I don't know. One of them was the Philippines consul general at the time, Buddy Gomez, who hated Marcos. I mean he was so vocal. I liked Buddy.

I showed the child abuse slides of Waiʻanae. Afterward, [Consuelo] shooed me out the door and said, "Tomorrow I'll let you know my decision." Then the next morning she called me—she's not a morning riser—she likes to sleep in: "Hello, dear. I have your first $15,000 check. Now how much is this shelter going to cost?" I gulped and said, "Fifty to $55,000 dollars per year, US." And she said, "Oh, I can manage that."

Consuelo was a very spiritual person, and this gave her a mission in life. This gave her purpose in life. She said, "You know dear, I love this. I love what I'm doing. I think I'd like to do this forever." That's when she said, "But I don't know how much I'm worth. I might be worth $7 million." She ended up leaving all of her shares to us, about 80 million shares in the Zobel family fortune. To that point, none of these shares had been sold outside the family. So it turned out to be someplace between $100 million and $150 million.

We established the Consuelo Foundation in July of 1988, and in 1989 she asked me to take it over. After twenty-three years with Child and Family Service I said, "Oh my goodness. You know what, I'm going to take the risk." I became president and CEO. She knew she had cancer, and she asked me in before the end of it.

This is a unique foundation. It's based on her love for the children and also for St. Thérèse of the Child Jesus, whose quotes are beautiful. One quote is, "I'm going to spend my heaven doing good on Earth." We always say that's what she's doing, you know? I mean hey, that's what she wanted, and that's what she's doing.

Q: *I understand the concept was to focus one quarter of the resources on Hawaiʻi and three quarters on the Philippines?*

Patti: That's right.

Q: *In the Philippines, you've done a lot of partnering in the areas of* *child protection and child abuse.*

Patti: Yes.

Q: *You returned to Wai'anae for your biggest project in Hawai'i.*

Patti: We did a survey: "What is the most critical need?" We found it was decent housing. Services were no longer lacking, which is good. Today the community has the Wai'anae Comprehensive Health Center, they have dental services, and even DHS goes out there if they have to.

The question was whether we could do anything about housing. Plenty of people said, "Oh, you're social workers. You don't know anything about doing housing. It's going to take six years to even get the permits." We had fourteen acres of land that a Catholic priest, Father Doherty, had found—"ag" land. We were going to have to get it rezoned for residential use, and a lot of people said, "Oh no, no, that you can't do." We went to the City Council, and I mean everybody was discouraging. Totally discouraging.

But again, there was this thing, "Never give up." We were the first one to get something called the 2OE waiver, which meant that you could more easily have the land reclassified from agriculture to residential. It took less than a year. Then the discouragement came around again: "You don't know about infrastructure."

I said, "We may learn some hard lessons, but we can learn how to do it." We did. After the first phase of the infrastructure, a part of the land was in a flood area, which our architect had not told us about, unfortunately. It cost us about half a million dollars, as I recall, because we had to bring in a lot of fill dirt.

Five hundred applied for the first increment. We did group sessions with them. We did role playing on family violence, role playing on child abuse, role playing on drugs. You know, what do you do if this or that happens with your neighbor? How do you handle this? And how do you handle that? In some ways it would be nice in a project like that, if they could all bond at once. We did a lottery at the end, and basically people were all happy with the houses.

As director of Child and Family Services, Patti lit the spark for development of the Consuelo Foundation, which provides services in Hawai`i and the Philippines.

Q: *How many families are there in the subdivision now?*

Patti: Seventy-five. Their houses were built for an average cost of about $55,000. We said that when they paid their mortgages off they could buy the land for another $70,000. That's about $130,000, and the houses are well worth $400,000. For the first twenty years, and until their mortgages are paid off, they must sell back to the Foundation [if they wish to move].

Q: *Is there a default history?*

Patti: The mortgage company foreclosed on only one family. In a default, the house will have to come back to us.

Q: *That's outstanding. One out of seventy-five over a twenty- to thirty-year horizon?*

Patti: It is.

Q: *I'm curious, in your journey did you struggle with cross-cultural issues, or cultural shock? If Wai`anae was a new culture, the Philippines was a very new culture.*

Patti: I didn't struggle that much with Wai'anae, and I didn't struggle that much in the Philippines. If there's something I really don't want to do that's a part of the culture, I'm real honest about it. "Thank you, but no thank you." Nobody seemed to hold that against me.

Q: *What do you tell young people starting out in social work?*

Patti: In schools of social work in the 1960s, the idea of objectivity trained social workers to adjust to systems. Today, thank God, we teach social workers that they must have some emotional involvement with their clients. We teach clients that they can and should change the systems that do harm. I recently taught a class at which I told them, "Don't ever give up being a change agent. You can make change happen. You can give hope where there is none. You can make the quality of life better for those with whom you come in touch. We can be proud to call ourselves social workers."

There's a story about Winston Churchill that describes his behavior during the bleakest, blackest hours of World War II. His people had to fight on if they were to survive as a nation. His jowls shook as he ended his speech with, "Don't ever give up." He turned to walk away from the podium, then he returned to say, "Don't give up." One more time he walked away, and one more time he returned and said, "Remember, don't ever give up."

Q: *That rallying call must apply to your health as well?*

Patti: Cancer has been a big part of my life. It's four different kinds of cancer in different parts of my body. I just found out that one in three women, *one in three*, will have a diagnosis of cancer in their lifetimes and one in two men, *one in two*, will have a diagnosis of cancer. One in five women will die from it and one in four men will die from it. I try to do the best I can to stay healthy and active.

Q: *After Child and Family Service, and after the Consuelo Founda-*

tion, you still can't escape your mission of responding to child abuse.

Patti: (Laughs.) I thought when I was retired I was never going to be involved in child abuse again. But one day I went to a meeting at the women's prison and as I was leaving a woman ran up to me in the inmate's uniform and said, "Hi. I'm the worst child abuser in Hawaiʻi. Would you please come to see me?"

I said, "I don't think I'm the one because I work with victims and not perpetrators." She threw her arms around me and she was crying. Then I asked her, "Who was the child?" I knew the case—a child who was beaten so badly that he was left blind and brain dead. I said to myself, "Oh my God no, I can't do this." That was 2010, and I still see the family. It's quite a family. She has served her twenty years and is off parole now. She's in school, she has a full-time job, and she is doing really well. I mean she has forgiven herself, I have forgiven her, she believes that God has forgiven her, and I think probably she is going to make it through. She wants to be a social worker, and we've got to see. She's fighting for it. ✦

CHAPTER 7

Andrew Chang

Andrew I. T. Chang was born in 1939 to an immigrant family, one of nine children. In college, he first majored in engineering. Through a process of soul searching, he departed from his father's guidance and studied social work. He approached his new profession based on a rapport with troubled teenagers and a classic casework orientation: "Start where your client is." The field was growing in the 1960s, and bright young people such as he were in demand. His horizons expanded rapidly into group work, community work, and then state government administration. He worked closely with the path-finding figures of the day, including Myron B. Thompson, Masaru Oshiro, and Richard Paglinawan. He played key roles in the administration of Gov. George R. Ariyoshi and then served as managing director of the City and County of Honolulu under Mayor Eileen Anderson.

Question: *Should we start with what led you to become a social worker?*

Andy Chang: Ah! (Chuckles.) To earn tuition, my summer job was working at the pineapple canneries, but I didn't want to do that anymore. I tried to get a job with "Parks and Rec" but they were full up. Then I got a call from a social worker at Salvation Army Children's Facility. She

(left) Andrew Chang, who abandoned the study of engineering for youth work, rose to the top reaches of both state and county government. (Above: Andy Chang with his daughter at a swearing-in ceremony.

said, "I understand you're interested in doing recreation work." Actually I had never thought of working at Salvation Army. "Just come in," she said. "Work for a week and if you don't like it, you can leave."

I fell in love with those kids. We got along famously well. They were on the borderline of going to what we used to call the Koʻolau Boys Home or the Girls Home. The judge would oftentimes say to them, "This is your last chance," and send them to Salvation Army Children's Facility. My job was to plan out recreation activities—take them to beaches, go on camping trips, et cetera. There was so much sadness in these kids, so many of them hurting, yet they were trying to do well. They were in a supervised home with people who loved them and they had the caseworkers who were trying to help them.

The Salvation Army was pure dedication. The administrator was a woman named Minnie Bell Shennan. She was a true Salvationist. She dedicated her entire life to the program. At the time, Pinky Thompson was director of social services and Larry Koseki was a case worker. I could see up close how they related to the kids. When you saw them hanging around, wanting somebody to talk to, you knew a kid was really in pain.

Q: *At that stage, were you thinking about social work as a career?*

Andy: Not yet. We grew up in a poor family. My parents were immigrants from China, someplace in Canton. There were six of us. Actually, there were nine of us. Three children were born in China, but they didn't make it for lack of health care. I learned about them because on one occasion my mother got to talking and she started to cry. That's when she told me we had three siblings who died in China. My father was back here in Hawai'i trying to earn some money to send home. But for some reason or another, she never got the money. I don't know whether the relatives intercepted it and then never gave it to her, but she couldn't get health care for the kids. I think that was the sadness and the tragedy in her life. She kept a lot to herself. But she was very strong. If there's anything the six of us learned, it was from her.

My mom used to describe me among the six by a Chinese term, *mow pi hi*, meaning I lacked patience. I would always speak up. If I thought there was an injustice done or I was accused wrongly, I would fight for my case. From the time I was little, I would never back away. (Chuckles.) My father felt the same way about me. I would always answer back. I couldn't sit quietly. I always had something to say, and sometimes they would take that as disobedience or insolence.

Q: *What about your dad?*

Andy: His mother gave birth to him here, and when he was maybe two or three years old, he went back to China with her. He lived there up through maybe ten or twelve years old, and then he came back here to work in his uncle's meat market on the Big Island. His job was to get up early in the morning, get things ready, and put the meat out onto the display window, and then he would go off to school. He got up to the third grade, and that was the end of it.

He worked hard. For a while he was a chauffeur for a very wealthy man in San Francisco. He liked to call himself a merchant, but he was largely a salesperson until he eventually opened his own little shop, which was a sundries and fountain in Kalihi. You know, malts, ice cream, candy, and off-the-counter type drugs. He's more of a quiet kind of guy, but he had an explosive temper. I would always try to understand why he got so pissed off. "Why are you so angry, Dad?" As my mom told us more about his life, I got to have some appreciation. He would wake up in the middle of the night screaming. In his nightmares he dreamed he had died and no one was taking care of the kids. He grew up when the Japanese invaded China and there was that fear. And there was also a fear that my mom, being an immigrant, would be shipped back to China and leave the six of us here with him. I realized he was always fearful about the future, and then I said, "Oh, that's why he had so short a fuse."

We never knew poverty *per se* because somehow he always managed to get a job. We were always fed. We lived in tenement housing, in what was known as Hell's Half Acre, close to ʻAʻala Park. It's where Kukui Gardens (urban renewal apartments) is today: 1248 Hall Street, no longer existing. There was a Buddhist temple in the back of our place, and—remember the Toyo Theatre? It was Japanese—it was within walking distance.

My dad wanted all of us to go to Catholic school, because he believed that nuns are better teachers, and initially, until the seventh grade, I went to St. Theresa's on School Street. Then we moved to Kaʻimukī, and I went to St. Patrick's and then St. Louis. The nuns were very supportive, and so were the brothers. But, you know, we were raised to be conformists, and so we conformed in school. As long as you behaved well, you got along pretty well with the teachers. (Chuckles.) And so I guess there was a reward that kept us in line.

Q: *So your dad struggled to take care of you as well as he did. And he wanted you to be an engineer. Solid employment, with a certain guaranteed level of status and income.*

Andy: That was 1957, the year the pioneering Russian satellite Sputnik went up. I was a senior in high school. Everybody wanted to be an engineer. My dad was delighted. He was really delighted. I was the only one who went away to school on the mainland because of that. He was willing to do the sacrifice that was necessary to send me away.

Toward the end of my junior year, my last quarter, I decided to take a course in psychology because I wasn't happy doing what I was doing.

I'll never forget my psychology professor. One day, she called me on the side and asked if she could speak personally. I said, "Yeah, sure." She asked, "What are you studying?" When I said engineering, she asked me, "Are you happy?" I said, "I guess so," which she questioned. "Are you sure?" She was picking up on my hesitance, and she convinced me to take a career-interest exam. When she looked at the results she said, "Engineering is not your lifetime profession. You belong in a helping profession." I said, "What am I going to do with all these science and math courses I've taken? What can I...?" She said, "Why don't you teach [those subjects]? That would get you engaged with people."

In those days you didn't call home often because of the cost, but I called home and told my parents I was getting out of engineering. I remember a deafening silence on my father's part. He didn't say a word to me.

At my summer job, the Salvation Army folks were suggesting I go to graduate school in social work. Larry Koseki took me under his wing, and after some urging Larry said, "Let's go do it. I'll write you up for a scholarship."[25] And that's how it got started.

Q: *Do you think the subterranean tragedies, such as from your three siblings who died, were part of what drew you to social work?*

Andy: I never thought about it that way, but who knows? Could be. Where does empathy come from? Where does caring for other people come from? My Mom was a very empathetic person. When I was a little kid, maybe seven or eight years old, a neighbor right across from us, a mother with seven kids, passed away. I remember Mother just crying, and crying, and crying for her and crying for the kids. She said, "Who's going to take care of them?" I can still picture myself in that tenement housing where she was standing, and where I was standing.

The dean of the School of Social Work conditioned my acceptance on taking courses in social sciences like sociology, criminology, and

---

25 Dr. Lawrence K. Koseki was an innovative and influential social worker of the 1960s and 1970s.

adolescent psychology. I spent a semester at UH taking undergraduate courses, and that qualified me into the School of Social Work.

Q: *Who did you think of as a major educational influence?*

Andy: I would say it was my professor for casework, a man named Fred Merritt. He began his lecture on the first day of class by writing on the board, "Start where your client is." At the time, people who went into social work were thinking they're going to solve the world's problems, right? So they know it all. But Fred Merritt took us to the fundamentals of casework. Casework is about your client. And you've got to start where they are if you're going to help them. If you start anywhere else, you're going to miss the target. You're not going to allow your client to share with you what he or she may be feeling. That lesson followed me throughout my work life.

Next is developing rapport and trust. If a client is really hurting, they don't want to be told what's wrong with them. They need someone to understand them and to understand where their pains are. They need rapport, they need trust, and a chance to be comfortable with themselves.

Introspection is important. With introspection, you can keep track of where you're coming from. You're less inclined to superimpose your own issues on someone else.

At the time (1963-64), the students were mostly interested in casework. Some of us went into psychiatric social work and some went into family counseling. One student might have been in group work, and I don't think there was a student that was enrolled in community organization as major coursework. For my master's degree research, my assignment was to do a study on Aid to Families of Dependent Children with unemployed parents. I would go out in the field to collect data. I spent time in Wai'anae on the leeward side and all the way up to Kahalu'u on the windward side. Back then, it was going out in the "boonies." Going up a dirt road, finding a home, was a task in itself. I still remember one man who refused to allow me into his home to be interviewed, so we agreed to meet across the street at the park. He was unemployed, and he was on public assistance. After talking to him, I learned he was ashamed of his state of affairs. He saw himself as a failure as a father, because he had his little kids to feed.

Andy Chang earned his master's degree in social work in 1964, the same year Congress passed the Economic Opportunity Act. Thereafter he served two years in the US Army in psychiatric social work. Returning to Hawai'i, he did four months of casework at Catholic Social Services, then set up a group home for the Salvation Army Boys Home. He then was invited to interview for a job as a field coordinator for the Honolulu Community Action Program (CAP), the community anti-poverty agency tasked with maximum involvement of its beneficiaries. The interviewer was the chairman of the CAP board, Peter Ka'aiali'i, a community leader from Nānākuli.

Andy: Peter said, "You've got your social worker degree. But what makes you think you can solve all the problems of poverty?" That threw me for a loop. I said, "I don't have a solution for poverty. I don't even know what's going on in the program in the first place, much less the people. So I have to understand that first before I can begin to have some inkling." Peter turned to the staff director—Wayne Omuro—and said, "Hire that guy."

A lot of people in the anti-poverty target areas were destitute. They were really poor. Crime rates were high. Health care was practically nothing. But there was a lot of excitement in the air. This was a "War on Poverty," right? There was a declaration by the president (Lyndon Johnson). I remember going to a national conference of OEO (Office of Economic Opportunity), where Vice President Hubert Humphrey was the lead agent for the president. Saul Alinsky, guru of community action, came into town, and one of our prominent participants declared himself to be a communist. Then there was Head Start. It was, to me, really exciting because of the requirement that you hire people indigenous to the area. Lots of the folks brought in to be aides were on public assistance, and Head Start gave them a sense of importance and purpose. You see women dressing up, looking very energetic, looking very happy with where they are and what they're doing.

It gave me a lift. There was a sense of idealism that many of us did not have—really, really have—until the War on Poverty came about. It took us to a higher level of how to make life better for people.

There was a lot of experimentation, and some of it paid off. I remember precisely what the salary was to entice a physician to go out to provide health care out in Wai'anae. It was $25,000. And so that's how health care got started out there. Then the School of Public Health went out and this eventually led to the Comprehensive Health Center in Wai'anae.

In 1971, only thirty-one years old, Andy Chang succeeded the late Paul Nakamura as the head of the State of Hawai'i Office of Economic Opportunity. Shortly thereafter, he was appointed deputy director of the Department of Social Services and Housing (DSSH), serving under none other than Myron "Pinky" Thompson. Funding and enthusiasm for the more activist War on Poverty programs were ebbing, but social justice work—through a network of social workers—was embedded at the top levels of Hawai'i's state government.

Q: *How was it — working with Myron Thompson?*

Andy: What a guy! A deep, thoughtful person. When he says something, you really know he's thought it through. He had a clear sense of what he wanted to do. Where some people just play the politics of the office, he took the office very seriously. He would say, "There are a lot of people out there who need help." His heart and his priorities were always about children and providing them the right environment to grow up to be healthy human beings. A lot of his ideas were driven by his concern for the well-being of children. I remember he became a source of controversy in the editorial pages when he advocated for the Food Stamp Program and why it was so necessary to get good nutrition into people, especially for children, because it affects their study habits. He says, "Why are people complaining? The Food Stamp money has a multiplier effect. It generates economic activity in the state, so we should be happy to get those dollars and take care of people." The critics jumped all over him, saying he didn't understand economics. But it was really true. When money flows into any jurisdiction, it generates business activity and taxes.

Pinky would come up with an idea and fly off to Washington, DC, to see if we could get federal funding. When he found a source, he would consult [US senator Daniel K. Inouye's chief of staff] Dr. Pat DeLeon on how to get the money for Hawai'i. Pinky would call in, and his secretary Lydia would pick up the phone and say, "Andy, it's Pinky on the line again." I would grab my notebook because he would be doing a lot of talking, and I was doing a lot of writing to make sure I followed up on his instructions. That's Pinky. He was always looking ahead, looking at how he can exploit the various resources that are available to help the people of Hawai'i. He came back with a lot of money through Senator Inouye's office, and in the process he developed a very close relationship with Senator Inouye.

He had a natural, empathetic ability about him. Social work was just a profession that helped him put it all together in a way that he could express himself.

At the same time, he was a simple, down-to-earth guy. He would say, "Hey, Andy, let's go out to lunch." So we would go to a restaurant on King Street where they served really terrific watercress pork with rice. When it came time to pay, he'd say, "Oh, Andy, let me get it." I would say, "No, no," but he would insist. He would reach for his back pocket and his wallet was totally empty. He would say with laughter, "My kids went through my wallet again without telling me."

After Lt. Gov. George R. Ariyoshi succeeded John A. Burns as governor, social workers continued to play important roles at a high level of state government. When Myron Thompson left the state to become a trustee of the Bishop Estate, Ariyoshi appointed Andy Chang to succeed him as head the Department of Social Services and Housing (DSSH). As a result of the liberal programs of the 1960s, the functions of DSSH had expanded from its days handing out welfare payments. It now oversaw Medicaid, Child Protective Services, and the State Corrections System, to name a few. Two prominent social workers served under Chang as deputy directors—Masaru Oshiro and Richard Paglinawan.

Q: *With social workers in key positions, did you have a sense that the spirit of idealism and fulfilling broad social goals was animating the state?*

Andy: I personally didn't think of it that way. I never aspired to be a person with a cause. Once I got into responsibilities, people that we've been talking about were there to help me think things through. Masaru helped me manage the corrections side and Richard was handling the public assistance side and the vocational "rehab."

Q: *What would you tell people about Richard Paglinawan?*

Andy: Richard was a gem—a real gem. He was a deputy at Hawaiian Homes Commission, right? And he was willing to come over to DSSH. He was a big force in resurrecting *ho'oponopono* and bringing it to the state government. Also during that period, I was having a hard time dealing with the National Welfare Rights Organization, which was very active in the community. They were down at the legislature, lobbying, and much of their lobbying basically had the effect of condemning DSSH. Richard had a calming effect. He would take the most upset and agitated people and bring them into his office. By that time, you know, they're all laughing. He was a social worker through and through.

Q: *And Masaru Oshiro? What was your perspective on his renowned opposition to capital punishment?*

Andy: We had a lot of escapes from the prison. I mean, the place was just terrible. A police officer was shot by one of the escaped inmates. Fortunately, he didn't die, but he was shot. In a moment of weakness and emotion, I was interviewed by a reporter, and I said, "I'm against capital punishment but in certain instances when an officer of the law is shot and killed, in those instances, I would support capital punishment." I regret what I said till this day. I may be overstating, but I've wondered whether I had some influence on Gov. Ariyoshi's thinking at that time.

Influential legislators were pushing capital punishment and Ariyoshi eventually agreed to a bill for execution of "cop killers." Masaru said, "I'm against it." The governor said, "You can be against it. You can go down and testify [against it]." Masaru more or less replied, "Sorry, I'm against it, but I'm not going down. Because how can I take from the hand that feeds me?" He resigned. It had such a tremendous impact on me. To this day, I will never forget Masaru Oshiro for the lesson he taught me.

Masaru Oshiro was followed as deputy director of DSSH by yet another remarkable social worker of the time, Dr. Lawrence Koseki, who at Salvation Army had encouraged a younger Andy Chang to try social work. Koseki conducted a study of capital punishment that strongly reinforced Oshiro's position. It showed that in the territorial period, those executed were disproportionately Filipino and Hawaiian. Thereafter the proposal for capital punishment was never seriously revived.

Q: *Generally, how would you characterize your experience with Gov. Ariyoshi?*

Andy: Very good. Gov. Ariyoshi delegated responsibility. He said, "You administer based on what you think is right and what the law says." In all the years that I spent in his administration—it spans about ten years—I cannot recall one time that the governor asked me to do something for political reasons. He was strictly saying, "I hired you because you should be running the department. I should not be running the department. If there's anything political that comes your way and gets in the way, then you send it to me." That's what he told me. So I never had to worry about political fallout.

There was a period in which we were getting heat in the legislature on the issue of child abuse. Patti Lyons was leading the charge. While the staff did not appreciate the criticism, I did not see her as a villain who acted irresponsibly. In fact, she clearly showed a deep concern over what was happening to children who were being abused. The department was after all charged by state law with the responsibility of protecting children, and we weren't doing a good job, albeit for a lack of resources or whatever. Patti was crying out for help. If we weren't listening or additional resources were not forthcoming, then what other alternative did she have but to go to those who had the authority to do the inquiry and provide the needed resources? I always thought that people like Patti were the conscience of our profession.

There is one more thing I want to share with you that had so much impact. In one of the cabinet meetings, I was asked by the governor to share what our department was concerned about. "Okay, Andy, your turn." I said that federal social security (Title XX) payments for social services were capped at a low amount, $8 million or so. But there was so much child abuse in military families that we were stretched beyond our limits. At the governor's direction, I presented this situation to Dan Inouye.

Lo and behold, I got a call from Col. David Peters of Sen. Inouye's staff saying, "The senator wants me to arrange a meeting for you with all of the top military brass in the state." And here I was, geez, I was just a young kid, and all the brass comes in, with all their stars and all that. The staff introduces us casually and says, "Andy, tell them your story." I was told it was the first time the generals had heard about the tremendous problems their families were experiencing in terms of child abuse. What Inouye wanted to do was start a demonstration program in Hawaiʻi. We got the first grant based in a military setting and it created a family service center. Great. For me, wow, that was a huge load off of us.

Years later, I was in Washington, DC, and Pat DeLeon said, "Sit down. You're going to like this." He pulled out a budget sheet and it showed—I forget now exactly—I think it was $450 million of budget for family counseling services for the military. I tell you, I really had goose bumps. And Pat said, "Andy, you remember how this all got started?" I said, "Oh, do I remember."

Between 1981 and 1985, Andy Chang served as managing director of the City and County of Honolulu under Mayor Eileen Anderson. Thereafter he went into the public affairs department of Hawaiian Electric Industries, rising to the position of vice president for external affairs before retiring in 2010.

Q: *You actually had a short run at hands-on social work and a long* *run at high-level management. Masaru said, "I was foremost a case-worker." What would you say to that?*

Andy: I totally agree with Masaru. Once you have those principles, how you relate to people and how you treat people, the caseworker in you never leaves you.

The lessons learned from social work definitely helped me through the work that I was doing. It's always better when you understand something, and it's good to understand that you don't understand something. Respect others. Try to get where they're coming from. Develop trust. Ethics and integrity should apply through all professions throughout life, and I think social work really emphasizes those qualities in its students.

The principles of social work have followed me all the way. You fundamentally come down to understanding where another person is coming from—understand why they take a position they're taking. You apply those skills, whether intuitively or otherwise. You don't think about it. It's just part of the process. It's part of your way of living your life. ✦

CHAPTER 8

Susan Chandler

When Susan Chandler interviewed to be director of the State Department of Human Services, Gov. Ben Cayetano wanted to know why Medicaid was costing the state government so much money. Susan went from explaining the complexities of health care systems to arguing for a bigger health care budget. On her return home, she told her husband the interview was an unqualified disaster. The telephone rang. "I like your spunk," the governor said. "I want to hire you."

Question: *Where to begin?*

Susan Chandler: You've been interviewing some good people, and I've been getting a little nervous. There are lots of themes in social work, so that is a struggle in itself. I keep returning to the theme of *empowerment*. I've tried to listen to people in such a way that they are really leading, and it's their interests that we're trying to move forward, not ours as professionals. Looking back, I see many opportunities to do this have landed in my lap.

Q: *In the beginning...*

Susan: My family lived in Scarsdale, New York, outside New York City.

It was very upper middle class. Everyone wanted to move there because of the excellent schools. My first venture into the real world was age fourteen or so—this was the 1950s. My father was an attorney for the Amalgamated Clothing Workers of America, which meant he worked with low-income people in New York City. A lot of workers were coming into the "needle trades" from Puerto Rico, and they didn't speak English very well. I volunteered to tutor them. I didn't know how to teach, but I could speak English and I learned a little Spanish. This was a matter of helping a group of people over the linguistic barrier, and it introduced me to a structural viewpoint, as opposed to individuals with problems.

When I went to Cornell University in the early 60s, I was again a tutor—tutoring isn't quite the word—for African American students from Harlem. It was almost like a socialization, helping people get a better understanding of how to work through an environment that's new to them. For example, I would talk about how to go to a faculty person and find out in advance what an exam was going to be like.

Q: *From there, how did your thinking about empowerment evolve?*

Susan: David (Chandler) and I had gotten married in August 1967, and he started teaching sociology at the University of Hawai'i in the fall semester. I was fresh out of undergraduate school at Cornell and didn't know anybody in Hawai'i. I had trained in psychology, and I wanted to work in what we used to call human resources. I liked the idea of helping people find jobs and do well in their jobs. I knew absolutely nobody, and I literally would knock on a door and say, "Can I have a job in human resources?" And they would say, "Well, who are you?" So that didn't work out very well. After weeks of being turned down, I heard about a project at the Social Science Research Institute at UH, where a sociology professor was writing a book on mental illness. He needed a graduate assistant. The idea was that mental illness was not a brain illness but is socially defined, or a socially constructed disease. For example, the rates of schizophrenia around the world are very different from place to place. The rate is much higher in cultures that don't toler-

Susan Chandler, Ph.D.—activist, social worker, scholar, and director of the State Department of Human Services.

ate certain kinds of deviant behavior, and it's lower in cultures that do.

In 1967 that was a fabulously interesting idea. I went into the State Hospital and interviewed people. I remember a woman whose husband decided she was crazy and he wanted to marry somebody else. So rather than go through a divorce he institutionalized her, which at that time you could do on one doctor's letter. I asked the nurse, why not lighten up on the woman's medication? And she said, "Oh, she'll just complain about everything." Even though the woman was only one person, there were plenty of others who had been defined as mentally ill and lost their rights. It was a very upsetting experience.

So mental health was my first step into social work. As a UH graduate student I joined the Mental Health Association and got into the question of whether there should even be a State Mental Hospital. I did my second-year practicum at the Youth Correctional Facility. I could see many of the kids had mental health challenges, but they were incarcerated because they had run away. Often these were not for serious crimes but they were stuck in the facility with indeterminate sentences. They got the incarceration treatment but not much in the way of mental health treatment.

This was how I got involved in reforming the law. Possibly because both my dad and my mom were attorneys, I had rights issues in my pablum. Among students at the School of Social Work, we had the Political Action and Public Affairs Committee—the PAPA Committee. Traditionally, a single doctor could write a note saying, "Yes, I think that person's crazy." Hawai'i then went briefly to a two-doctor routine, but in the early 1970s we became one of the first places to have due process. This meant that someone or some entity had at least to go to court before a person was involuntarily committed, and a person had the right to counsel and to explain their side of the story.

Today, some people think deinstitutionalization has gone way too far, that you can't commit an individual to an institution who badly needs the help, such as mentally ill people on the streets who don't want to take their "meds."

Q: *That's a tough issue.*

Susan: It's a very tough issue.

Q: *How did your student activism relate to your studies?*

Susan: The year I graduated, 1970, about seventy-five students were in clinical social work and only five of us were interested in community organization, or what they called "macro" (as opposed to "micro") social work. The five of us had separate classes. We wrote grants and became quite active. We went to the Faculty Senate and said, "The school shouldn't require us to take all these clinically oriented classes. Why can't we take classes in political science and sociology instead?" We did get a little bit of flexibility in the curriculum. We sort of won the battle but lost the war, because we alienated a lot of the faculty in the process.

Q: *In your School of Social Work years (1968-1970) the War on Poverty was struggling to continue as a vital program. Did this have an effect on you?*

Susan: It had a big effect. At UH, we went out into the community. We worked in Pālolo Housing. I did my master's thesis at Kūhiō Park Terrace (public housing in Kalihi), looking at the question of why people in low-income communities aren't more politically active. I was framing my questions in terms of, "How come you don't go to the legislature like I do? How come you don't do this, that and the other thing?" It was quite a rude phrasing, and I was called on it by people who said, "What do you know about what we do? What do you know about the politics we're active in?"

That was a big learning experience right there. Their issues were different; their community structures were different; and their leadership was very different. So I was some little white kid who's twenty-three years old landing on their structures. It was pretty awful. Even though I already had the empowerment idea in my head, I didn't practice it very well in the early days.

I wasn't trying to be a rabble rouser, but I remember going to a lecture by the community organizer Saul Alinsky at the Church of the Crossroads here in Honolulu in 1972. His book *Rules for Radicals* had become pretty basic reading for me. I liked the way he thought about power struggles. It wasn't like I was becoming a communist, and it wasn't anti-government as much as it was thinking about techniques that people can use to get better wages. Saul Alinsky did creative kinds of strikes. In Rochester (New York), the Kodak camera company never hired Black people, even though the community was about twenty-five percent Black. So his technique was to get lots of Black people to shop in the camera stores and load up goods from the store but then not buy. They weren't doing anything illegal, but it was upsetting to the store managers. They told other people who told other people who eventually got to Kodak, and they worked out a quota, and at least they were bringing in Blacks to get jobs. So there were subtle community actions that oftentimes were pretty creative and sort of fun and pounded away at the power structure.

As Alinsky talked, I thought I wanted to work in Chicago. I started talking to him, and he said, "Tell me a little about your background. Where're you from?" New York, I said. He said, "No, I mean, really. Where are you from?" I didn't want to say Scarsdale because I figured that put me outside of anything. When I finally did he said, "You can't work *with* a community until you've worked *in* a community. So you can't be a community organizer if you don't know anything about the community. Live in a place five years and then call me."

Q: *What were some of your next markers?*

Susan: Well, the first job I got after the School of Social Work was a strange thing. It was with a federally funded state agency that was interested in youth problems and interfaced with the county police departments. I was called the Statewide Coordinator of Youth, a pretty fancy title for not much of a job.

Those were the days when you were trying to bring delinquents into the power structures of decision-making around youth programming. I went to different schools across the state. I learned all kinds of things about Kaua'i and Moloka'i. I talked with teachers about their struggles with the various kids, and actually they had things like the Alienated Youth Club, a club for kids who didn't want to go to other clubs.

I wrote a statewide plan for helping kids who weren't doing well in school as kind of a drug prevention thing. Then I met with the chiefs of police and the law enforcement people and the social workers and the teachers. I thought it was an interesting paper about how to include kids in discussions and how to do after-school programs that would better relate to the kids' interests. When I gave it to my boss, I was naive enough to believe they were gonna do something with it.

He said, "No, we're not going in that direction anymore." They didn't change directions very subtly. They put all of the money that was supposed to be in youth services into a riot truck in Honolulu. A thing with guns and stuff. It seemed to me they could at least have said, "Thank you." I quit.

Q: *The idea behind talking with the kids was inspired by the anti-poverty concept of "maximum feasible participation" of those who are served.*

Susan: That's right. Exactly. That sounded terrific.

Q: *Did you hear that a lot?*

Susan: Yes.

Q: *And you attempted to practice it?*

Susan: Yes. My second job was in Wai'anae. It was part of a Community Action Program, and it was all about "maximum feasible participation." The community people had all the political skills they needed, but I made myself useful by translating their ideas into grantsmanship language. They had all the ideas and I could format them to get funding from the Feds. I was called a community health planner. I was the "go to" girl, the scribe. I took minutes of meetings. Even a simple thing like that was empowering, because it meant subsequent meetings would move forward.

I was amazingly well-tolerated. I was a kid from New York, and this was seeing the underside of Wai'anae. I remember sitting there with a particular community leader. She opened her purse to take out a cigarette and there was a gun. I'd never seen a gun in my life. The people were very protective. If anyone got a little nasty, someone would say, "Hey, she's helping us." It was like they were tapping the top of my head. "Come on, sweetie, come and sit down. Would you like some food?" They always made me feel like I was participating at some level for good things.

At the time, there was no health care on O'ahu past Pearl City, and my task was to help them develop a health center. I had been taught how to write a grant in social work school, but I'd never really done it. But, yeah. I wrote grants for them. And the thing that was crazy, I was now twenty-four and I wrote a $350,000 grant to set up planning for health services.

The ideology of "maximum feasible participation" really did change how the Wai'anae Health Center was built and structured. It has a community board. They hire the doctors. I remember a big, long discussion about whether doctors should have staff bathrooms or whether they should have the same bathrooms as everyone else. The board decided, why should doctors have a better bathroom than the clients?

Q: *By that point, how were you feeling about the idea of maximum feasible participation of the beneficiary group?*

Susan: I loved the idea. It fit exactly as I would want it to. But I also saw power dynamics that weren't as fabulously equitable as I expected. Again, I was pretty naive. I thought if you turn all this money and power over to a community, the community is going to be open to everyone. But it really wasn't.

Certain people in the community were very strong and dominant. They weren't letting younger people or new people come in. So it wasn't the most diverse group.

Q: *Prosaically, these were the neighborhood politicians.*

Susan: Some of whom became state capitol politicians after that. I'm not suggesting it was corrupt. Their dream was to improve the community. It just wasn't particularly participatory. Nonetheless, good things happened.

I worked three years in that program and I was there the day they broke ground for the Wai'anae Coast Comprehensive Health Center. This was pretty heady. So I feel that if my first job was a failure, this second one worked.

Q: *Did you run across Patti Lyons in the process?*

Susan: I knew Patti, yes. She was at Child and Family Service, and I thought of her as a sort of heroine for her work on child abuse.

Q: *One last question about Wai'anae: How important was the Economic Opportunity Act of 1965 as an impetus for activity?*

Susan: Tremendously important.

Q: *By this time, it was 1973 and you were twenty-eight or so.*

Susan: Yes. This was my husband David's first sabbatical year, and he had the opportunity to teach at [the University of California] Berkeley. It was a chance to put my education and his sabbatical in the same place, so I started my Ph.D. program there.

Q: *How would you describe the influence of David?*

Susan: He was Canadian and pretty leftist politically. Sensibly, I think. He worked in the steel mills. He was very, very, very smart, so he became a teaching assistant at Cornell. He was in the Ph.D. program there when I was an undergraduate. He was interested in cross-cultural ethnic marriages and marriage stability. Ethnic in those days for a Canadian was

French marrying English. How many French were marrying English? That was seen as inter-ethnic marriage. A famous sociologist said to him, "If you're gonna really look at anything ethnic you should move to Hawai'i for a year," and that was when he got a teaching job in sociology. When it looked like the legislature might pass a death penalty bill here, he got deeply involved in fighting it. We had people at our house all the time and he was well-acquainted with Masaru Oshiro's views, for example. That was his deeper entrée into Hawai'i and then he got interested in mediation and conflict resolution and he was a founder of the Neighborhood Justice Center.

Q: *What were your intellectual parallels with David?*

Susan: David was also a structuralist. I was very taken with that and when I went to the doctoral program I wanted to be able to think like that and do that kind of work—but never leaving the activist side.

Q: *At Berkeley you studied primarily community organization?*

They called it policy. They called it macro social work. But the people that I worked with wrote the books on community organizing. I was on a National Institute of Mental Health grant and I had to then commit to working on something about mental health. So I again worked on interviewing people coming out of mental hospitals, only this was California. The question was social integration of mental health clients. Were they being accepted into a community? They weren't. They were living in houses with caregivers and never even went out of the house.

You just asked simple questions. "Have you ever been to the library? Have you ever been shopping?" Nothing. This was like living in a little institution. So that whole community mental health movement wasn't working well in California. It was described in law as deinstitutionalization, but it was really a precursor to homelessness now—at least that's what I think.

I came back to Hawai'i as a result of bumping smack into [UH professor of social work] Oscar Kurren at a ballet in San Francisco. He asked what I was working on, and then he suggested I work with him and finish my doctorate at UH, and that's how I got into the UH School of Social Work. He hired me on a community mental health grant that was about mental patients connecting with the community and also getting their families listened to by psychiatrists. After three years, I moved into a real faculty position.

Q: *What would you say were the most important points of your teaching career?*

Susan: I like to feel I influenced students to think more broadly about themselves as practitioners and also the client base they are serving. I said to them, "I know you want to help people, but let's also ask why you think clients are in their particular situation? What's behind it? What are the policies that are not working so well for them?" We used to say that unfortunately the best clinicians move up in a social service agency and end up becoming policy people or administrators or political advocates. So the "micro" students as well as the "macro" students need policy skills.

In my community organization class, students had to go to the legislature. They had to really testify. The first year I did this, half the students said, "Oh, but the bill I was following died, so I can't go." I changed the rules of the class to say, "Too bad if your bill dies. Pick another one." It provided practice in advocating for people.

Susan's role as a professor of social work was interrupted by a career detour in 1995 that resulted from her being asked to interview with then governor-elect Benjamin J. Cayetano.

Susan: I interviewed him once on a study that I had done about after-school programs, but he didn't remember that. So, no, I didn't know the (new) governor. He was like, "Oh, my God. What am I gonna do? I don't know anybody who wants this job." He kept asking people, "Who's interested in social policy?" and my name would come up. I got a phone call that I thought was a joke: "Governor Cayetano would like to speak with you." And I said, "Oh, yeah? Okay. Hi." He started asking me all the questions. And as an academic I'm interested in explaining things. He wanted to know why Medicaid was so expensive. "Why are we spending all this money on Medicaid?" That was the interview question. I said, "Because we have a lot of people who don't have health insurance. And without it they aren't able to go to the doctor in a timely way."

He was wanting to find ways to cut costs on Medicaid services, and so we had a big argument. He telephoned me a little later and said, "I like your spunk. I'm gonna hire you. And if you make mistakes, that's okay as long as they're on behalf of people. But don't lie and don't get in trouble."

In the footsteps of Myron Thompson and Andrew Chang, Susan Chandler became the third professional social worker since statehood to head the Department of Human Services. For two gubernatorial terms (1995-2003), she experienced a mutually supportive relationship with Cayetano.

Susan: He was a kid from Kalihi, and he understood what it's like to be poor. At the beginning we were riding through an economic recession, and everybody but me (Human Services) had to cut their budgets. The rest of his cabinet officers would say, "Hey, how come Susan's not getting cut and everybody else is getting cut?"

With her roots in the anti-poverty movement, and also academia, she approached culturally based programming with caution.

Susan: The War on Poverty was very important in terms of impetus. Then influences came together to animate Hawaiians and Hawaiian culture. In the early days of my teaching, 1976 or so, you weren't supposed to make the point that the underclass in Hawai'i was disproportionately Hawaiian. The concept was, "Let's wipe out poverty." I am an empiricist, a scientific social worker. I believe there should be empirical research supporting treatment interventions.

So, for me, it took a while to watch that change from empowerment of the poor to empowerment resulting from the Hawaiian community

Susan with Gov. Benjamin J. Cayetano and her husband, David Chandler, a longtime UH professor of sociology.

saying, "We want things differently." Personally, I was at the back or late end of that shift. I don't think I got really conscious of that change until maybe the late '80s, or early '90s. In DHS, there was a huge issue of Hawaiian disproportionality in welfare programs, Medicaid programs, and child welfare programs. In all sorts of indicators, Hawaiians were way over-represented. I mean, why would seventy-five percent of the kids in foster care be Hawaiian when at most they represented twenty percent or so of the population? For years that kind of data was a secret. You weren't allowed to collect that kind of data. You weren't allowed to look at that kind of data. You weren't allowed to know that, even though people knew it.

I watched, and I slowly came to recognize the efficacy of the [*hoʻoponopono*] model of Lynette and Richard Paglinawan and their work and their abilities. I knew Lynette from the School of Social Work. I came to see *hoʻoponopono* as an indigenous practice that had a lot of applications.

In the early phase of practice, only Hawaiian people did it. You couldn't observe it. You couldn't be a part of it. And it had that religious orientation to it. To move it into the DHS bureaucracy like I did required special practitioners. I had to do it very carefully, and I spoke to Lynette and Richard a lot about it. I wanted to understand which pieces you could use and respect. I didn't want to offend anyone but I wanted to use the benefits among Hawaiians and non-Hawaiians alike.

The adaptation became known as the Ohana Conference program.

Susan: It was a model based on respect for the family and empowerment of the family. I would sit in Ohana Conferences where the people were speaking a language I had never heard. I had no idea what they were saying, and yet there was an energy that you could feel in the circle. So I believe it was a form of decision making and rehabilitation—restoration—that is really crucial. We weren't supposed to be praying because it was a government program. We would be at Zippy's or a place like that, and oftentimes the family wanted to start with a prayer, and everybody held hands in a circle and put their head down and prayed—and it was perfectly fine, whatever language they prayed in or whatever they were thinking about.

Q: *And is it ongoing?*

Susan: The Ohana Conferencing program is still going—oh yes! I think it changed the orientation from social workers saying, "You're a bad family and you've got to do X, Y and Z." The question became, "Who in your family can help? Where are the support systems in your family and in your community?"

I want to add one thing. I went to New Zealand in 1995—twice actually—and saw how the Maori group does it. There are a lot of similarities, except they have a law describing it, whereas ours is still a practice.

Q: *You're the data person. Do you have data on the effectiveness of the program?*

Susan: Yes, I do. I've written a lot about it. Maybe it's not the most perfect science but empirically I think it's quite good.

Q: *Is there a "next big thing" emerging that is vaguely comparable in impact to the anti-poverty initiative or the Hawaiian movement?*

Susan: Something different? The next one?

Q: *Is there something we haven't talked about?*

Susan: I've been in public administration the last ten years and I think the answer is sustainability of the environment and climate change. The environment can connect to Hawaiian stewardship of the land and water, and I think all of that is the next big issue both here and in the world.

I don't know where the field of social work comes in particularly, but I think of such questions as: What will happen to the environmental migrants? Where will they go when the islands start sinking and Africa dries up and you've got huge movements of people? Migrants of disaster. We as a world will have to think hard about it. ✦

PART III

A Contemporary Framework

CHAPTER 9

Observations

The previous eight stories cover nearly a century of Hawai'i's history. Without attempting to infer too much, I think they clearly show that social work matters. Where would we be without a Clorinda Lucas, an AQ McElrath, a Pinky Thompson, a Masaru Oshiro, or a Patti Lyons? Each combined compassion with training. Each made the most of opportunities at hand. Like steersmen in a canoe, they understood the waves, which in their storied lives were the New Deal, the organized labor movement, statehood, the Great Society, and the revitalization of Native Hawaiian life. Just as they were entwined across generations, so likewise the underlying forces of change were interrelated.

If the New Deal of the 1930s or the Hawai'i dock strike of 1949 may seem to some readers like ancient history, statehood in 1959 remains a more obvious pivotal point. When I was writing about state government for the newspapers in the late 1960s, one of my certainties was, "All paths lead to the capitol." When the survey researcher James Dannemiller summarized his work from the 1970s and 1980s, he said the large majority of Hawai'i's people had one response to questions of problem-solving. It was, in James's words, "The State, the State, and the State." Poll numbers for trust in state government ran high.

In the years since, the fervor for state government has declined. The perceived efficacy of the state government has drifted. In this third decade of the twenty-first century, many of Hawai'i's citizens, if interested at all, would agree that the State of Hawai'i has gone from one of the most actively progressive of the fifty states to one of caution and, where money is involved, conservatism. Social work and social justice no longer figure prominently in the capitol conversation.

In 2009, I was asked to speak at the public gathering marking fifty years of statehood. The event was originally advertised as a celebration. As planning for it progressed, it was renamed an observance, and it proved to be an observance that was short on joy. I said, "As we in Hawai'i start the next 'X' number of years of US statehood, most will agree the original invention is in trouble." I cited "myriad cascading problems: fiscal, educational, economic, etc. We have a resource management crisis, an energy crisis, and a crisis of leadership so pervasive in all sectors that it goes unremarked." This was published in the first of the three-part book series *Value of Hawai'i*, in which Susan Chandler undertook a more specific analysis of trends in social services. The State of Hawai'i, she wrote, "is cutting deeply into its public and private sector social services programs, and the cuts have been severe and broad-based. Hawai'i is withdrawing its historical commitment to provide an adequate safety net of health and social services."

Further, "Social services in Hawai'i have become a fragmented array of underfunded programs."

She placed this in the context of an American social welfare philosophy "structured to help as few people as possible for the shortest amount of time possible...problems are viewed as mistakes of individuals who didn't plan well enough or didn't work hard enough."[26]

The political culture of Hawai'i increasingly has exhibited broad trends of the other forty-nine states—such as pay-to-play fundraising, steeply rising campaign costs, tax breaks for the wealthy, stagnating minimum wage standards, reduced general welfare payments—the list runs on. Such causal factors are coupled to polarization, in Hawai'i's case not polarization between the Democratic and Republican parties, but—in the context of a virtually one-party political environment—

---

26 *Value of Hawai'i, Knowing the Past, Shaping the Future*, Craig Howes and Jonathan Kay Kamakawiwo'ole Osorio, editors (Honolulu, University of Hawai'i Press, 2010), 117-118

between the executive and legislative branches. Where the chief executive and legislature once worked more or less smoothly and effectively together, the two branches are now often at odds. This environment is also characterized by related phenomena such as ethical violations despite adequate ethics laws; and diminished transparency for the public despite adequate sunshine laws.[27] One striking symptom of such practices was the legislature's increasing reliance on a tactic called "gut and replace," meaning the late-moment wholesale change of one bill's content for another, without the benefit of a full public hearing. The 2021 session of the State Supreme Court, in a startling three-to-two decision, ruled the practice unconstitutional—a step by the third branch of government into legislative prerogatives that in past times would have been unthinkable. As this book goes to press, two members of the legislature recently have pleaded guilty to accepting bribes, and a legislative committee is busily drafting reform proposals.

The political environment and underlying social environment is a puzzle. Two questions often arise: "What's wrong with today's leadership?" and "Why can't Hawai'i do big things anymore?" For example, more than a half century after Head Start, why has the State of Hawai'i not provided preschool for all? Or, another example, why are general assistance payments to the most needy actually lower than they they were in the 1980s? Such questions are especially perplexing in light of the fact that much of today's government leadership appears to be well-meaning, more formally educated than their elders, and at least vaguely progressive, most consistently on issues having to do with tolerance. While the picture is not entirely bleak, particularly in the areas of gender and racial equity, a trend line is visible through the haze. It is about a decline in social consciousness, social activism, and political awareness since the mythologized 1960s. It is not for nothing that our social work group has worried about the level of devotion to social justice.

27 For example, as I write, Common Cause Hawai'i has produced a discussion paper raising the "process" issues above.

THE UP/DOWN ARC OF I-WE-I

This picture may strike us less personally and less parochially if we consider it in context of the United States as a whole. One of the foremost scholars of US trend lines, Robert D. Putnam, has produced the useful book *The Upswing*. It covers not only the six decades since the 1960s but the six previous decades—that is, it runs parallel to Hawai'i's entire experience since America's 1898 takeover.

From his data-mining, Putnam traces four currents running through this stream of American time. These are (1) economic disparities; (2) what he calls "comity and compromise" in politics; (3) social cohesion; and (4) altruism. He begins in the Age of the Robber Baron, a time characterized by economic and social disparity. This period, the early twentieth century, coincides with the political power of Hawai'i's white oligarchy and the economic dominance of the Big Five corporations. It is Putnam's initial "I," as in a social attitude that revolves around "I, I, I, me, me, me."

Next in Putnam's history comes a long transition through World War I, the New Deal, and World War II, up into the 1960s. He contends that life is less and less about "me," and more about "we." Contrary to most standard narratives, he presents extensive data supporting significant African American progress in spite of segregation and Jim Crow violence.

The question for Hawai'i is, what was going on during this period of territorial government? Much of what comparatively little is known about territorial Hawai'i between annexation and statehood tends to be either romanticized nonsense or—an opposing view—a biting critique of the racial and class hierarchy of the industrial plantation system. Without setting out to do so, my research for a recent book titled *Inclusion* wandered into a paradox like Putnam's. That is, within Hawai'i, while the ills of the *rural* plantation system continued more or less intact until after World War II (parallel to Jim Crow), *urban* Hawai'i was developing a more progressive society. Beginning in the 1910s, up into the onset of World War II, various individuals and institutions began to consciously work at navigating across ethnic and social boundaries. The kindergarten and settlement-house movements took hold. Ethnic and then inter-ethnic YMCAs proliferated. Junior high schools and high schools sprouted. The University of Hawai'i added thought-provoking new programs. A pan-Pacific internationalism became a kind of mania. Civic associations such as Rotary and Lions spread. Most explosively for the future, radical labor organizers developed bases of influence.

Accelerated by the shared hardships of World War II, these factors came together during the late 1940s and early 1950s in political upheaval, mass labor strikes, the passage of statehood, and the reforms of the early statehood period.

In Putnam's analysis of the country, his "We" period—the high point of shared economic progress, political cooperation, and social cohesion—similarly was the mid- to late-1960s. This was followed by a long downhill drift.[28] The presidential emblems of the downhill trend are Richard Nixon, Ronald Reagan, George H. W. Bush, George W. Bush, Donald Trump, and, to a lesser extent, the conservative Democratic streak at work in the presidencies of Jimmy Carter and William Clinton. In other words, Putnam's I-We line bends back down to I. As a graph, it looks like a mountain, running up to a peak and back down to the plain. *I-We-I.*

The trend lines of the United States as a whole and that of the *state* government of Hawai'i have a roughly similar shape. The qualifier, I submit, is that Hawai'i's period of active social consciousness and reform lasted longer. While the US turned heavily Republican after the 1968 election, Hawai'i continued as a Democratic Party state, albeit through an increasingly numbing one-party system. One bookend is the liberal State of Hawai'i constitution written and adopted in 1978.

But give or take a margin for argument, many observers would agree that Putnam's I-We-I arc for the United States is at least partially shared by Hawai'i. Put another way, Hawai'i's socioeconomic and political history—which we like to think of as being so uniquely our own—

---

28 Robert D. Putnam, *The Upswing: How America Came Together a Century Ago and How We Can Do it Again* (New York, Simon & Schuster) 205-207. He cites data to the effect that the lessening disparity in longevity between whites and blacks, after improving, has returned to its 1960 level. The gap in infant mortality actually has widened. The disparity between white and black family incomes is nearly the same, and so on.

has become more and more influenced by the American nation that absorbed Hawai'i in 1898.

If this observation is accurate, the combined federal/state question for social justice initiatives, and even for our society as a whole, is whether we are starting an upswing, or whether we are going to drift further downward. Are we citizens of a society in which everyone is out for themselves, or a society in which people exhibit an operative concern for one another?

THE NATIVE HAWAIIAN COUNTERTREND

With that issue left hanging, the question remains: how is Hawai'i different from the rest of the United States, as many of us believe, or at least would like to believe? The most obvious departure from the I-We-I story is that the Hawaiian community has maintained an upward trajectory since the 1970s. Across a half-century revival of Hawaiian life, cultural practices have been revalued and normalized. Suppressed history has been unearthed. Native Hawaiians—in nationalist terms, the Hawaiian *lāhui*—have made hard-won gains in the reform and expansion of social services, education, health care, and employment training. A system of Hawaiian immersion schools has been established. The Hawaiian language has been rescued from the brink of extinction, and bilingualism is rapidly growing. Ancient voyaging by non-instrument navigation has been revived. Indigenous rights have been codified in the State of Hawai'i's constitution. Kamehameha Schools has been transformed from a largely industrial trade school to a contemporary college preparatory school. Thanks in part to Pinky Thompson's impact as a trustee, its educational programs begin in the cradle and run up through support for advanced academic degrees. Finally, land and near-shore waters are being reclaimed and restored to health in efforts that more often than not are led by Native Hawaiian sweat-labor and passion for sustainability.

THE FUTURE

All of this raises questions about how social work might continue to evolve and how social justice might be defined and pursued. Will the Hawaiian movement prove to be predominantly inclusive or predominantly based on *koko* (blood)? To what extent will Hawaiians, followed by non-Hawaiians, buy in to the culture, tenets, and practices of a revived lāhui? What, if any, accommodation will the US federal government and the state government make to this submerged nation? Will the injustices of the past be seriously addressed, or will they continue to fester?

Inescapably, the issues of Hawai'i and the United States are intertwined. Will the progressive movement in the United States be successfully revived? Putnam, for his part, believes this is an imminent possibility, hence his title *The Upswing.* In 2020, a president who caricatured the Gilded Age was voted out in favor of one who leads with empathy. President Joe Biden has presented an agenda of expanded health care, support for childcare, an end to child poverty, expanded subsidies for education and other safety-net concepts. If successful, these programs could create a wave like that of the New Deal in the 1930s or the Great Society in the 1960s. Will today's young social workers recognize the opportunity, and will they make the most of it? ✦

CHAPTER 10

Student Voices

The size and composition of the new generation of social workers is changing rapidly. In addition to the longstanding UH School of Social Work, Hawaiʻi Pacific University and Brigham Young University–Hawaiʻi have developed degree-granting programs. Where Pinky Thompson was said to be the only Native Hawaiian student of his time, about one-third of today's UH social work students are Native Hawaiians and Pacific Islanders. Where he was one of thirty social work students in the early 1950s, today there are around four hundred at UH alone. Two hundred fifty or so are in the master's program and another one hundred forty to fifty are in the bachelor's program. Twenty or so are working on doctorate degrees.

As for Pinky Thompson's belief that the spirit of aloha can change the world, the social work school's website is in fourteen languages, including not only English and Hawaiian but Afrikaans, Arabic, Filipino, French, Hindi, Japanese, Korean, Maori, Mongolian, Samoan, and Spanish. The concepts of cultural validation, biculturalism, multiculturalism, and cultural competence are being worked and reworked. To the extent these ideas are spreading, it seems plausible that Hawaiʻi's version of social work is having an impact around the globe.

The very act of naming the flagship school for an indigenous leader tells a story. In its statement of guiding values, the Myron Thompson School of Social Work describes *hoʻokaulike*, justice, as paramount. Further, "[a]s a community of social workers and educators, we are committed to...challenge the status quo, advocate for social justice [and] fight against racial, xenophobic, [and] sexual violence in our society."

The social work school has been merged with the university's public health program, reflecting a broad definition of well-being that Pinky Thompson nurtured through his congressional initiatives. With the addition of public health majors, the student body nearly doubled in size, to around seven hundred.

As a result of long-term advocacy by the Hawai'i chapter of the National Association of Social Workers, the 1994 legislature adopted a social worker licensing law, creating three categories: bachelor of social work, master of social work, and clinical social work. The impetus for the law was to recognize social work as a profession, set standards, and facilitate third-party insurer payments for private practitioners. Its definition brings to mind the way in which the profession is about so many things—"applying the formal knowledge base, theoretical concepts, specific functional skills, and essential social values to effect change in human behavior, emotional response, and social conditions, and helping individuals, couples, families, groups and community organizations enhance or restore their capacities for personal and social functioning while preventing and controlling social problems."[29]

STUDENT VIEWS

To explore our group's concern for social justice work, we invited students to volunteer for round table conversations. We sought insight into the question that first motivated our project: Is the ideal of social justice still burning? If so, is it down to embers? Or has it burned out? These discussions systematically revolved around the students' career decisions, their sense of the present, and their hopes for the future. Dr. Susan Chandler asked students to open their minds and hearts, and to rest assured that their identities would not be disclosed. Their stories ranged widely, but as a common denominator the concept of social justice was alive and well in their studies, their practicum experiences, and

---

29 Hawai'i Revised Statutes 466-E-1

their conversation.

Several students framed social work as a calling with these words: *We don't choose it. It chooses us.* We saw several instances where the spark or focus particularly seemed to be coming from Native Hawaiians, who in turn inspired or challenged other students. For starters, it was Native Hawaiians along with Pacific Islanders who disproportionately showed up, answering the call for participants. For sheer grit, a young woman nearing her master's degree in social work was particularly memorable. She commuted from Wai'anae to Mānoa. She worked a full-time job while carrying a nearly full load as a student. As a child she had been orphaned by the death of her parents and then, effectively, orphaned a second time by the death of her grandparents. She was put into a foster care home, where she witnessed domestic violence and other forms of abuse. "And my brother went into his own drug world," she went on with her story, "and that causes a lot of trauma in my life. But despite all the problems I found myself always helping people. My social worker over at [Lili'uokalani Trust] said, 'You might be good at social work.' And when I went to the School, [Professor] Mike DeMattos, one of my faves, gave us that quote, 'We don't choose social work. It chooses us.'

"I'm learning about the healing process as I go, but I connect with the families and understand a lot of what they're going through. I love this field. Being a social worker is not just about social work. It's about everyone and everything."

In the discussions, cultural competence was a big subject. One of the students said: "Sometimes we come from a Western model of social work that can actually hinder our ability to help families or individuals because they have a different set of standards and beliefs. We're like, 'This is supposed to help. Why isn't this helping?' But it's because we're not looking at the cultural aspects, and that's why cultural competence is so important in the diverse communities in which we work. That is the most important value: Competence, culturally and professionally."

For students from elsewhere, education in Hawai'i is a wake-up call. A female from the US continent said: "When I came here I thought of Hawai'i as a paradise. Now I see we need to get everyone on the same page and realize this is a Hawaiian place. We need to respect it."

A Pacific Islander student said: "It's empowering for me to see Hawaiians are making progress. They want to move faster, [and] it's reason for optimism. I've taken from them as cousins. My long-term goal is equality in all aspects."

Outsized ambitions occasionally emerged: "I want to work towards free health care and free state colleges. I also want to work towards a resource-based economy."

A step-by-step view was more common: "I don't know that we would be here if we weren't optimistic about changes that we can make. It's a matter of working at a grassroots level with people to recognize they can voice their concerns. We can help them empower themselves. If we do, social justice will happen from the ground up—*from* the people themselves, rather than us making changes *for* people." Similarly: "We can find something we're really passionate about and we just keep working on it. We can't really think about changing things on a macro level. But making these small changes, micro changes, eventually will lead to bridging and to partnerships and having everyone collectively work to make change on a macro level."

A more skeptical view was never far away: "Social work is a constant uphill battle. Our teachers tell us our goal is to work ourselves out of a job, but that will never happen."

There was also an awareness that social workers are often taken for granted: "I see us social workers down in the bowels of the ship just plugging those little holes. You don't really know we're there, but imagine if we weren't there. Little menehunes. If you looked at all the good things we do, it would fill the Sunday paper."

MICRO AND MACRO

Paradoxically, social justice is continuously taught as a basic dimension of social work, yet most of the practice revolves around treating individual hurts and wounds. From this, social work professionals talk about a "micro" approach versus a "macro" approach—or casework versus community work. In the actual doing, it seems more accurate to say that young social workers set out with the open-ended goal of helping others and may or may not progress to broader public problems, public issues, and public causes. The root is a concern for humanity.

At UH, Professor Mike DeMattos teaches a course on "human behavior," a subject of wide range and flexible definition. A central message of his class is that social work methodology is applicable to individuals, groups, and society in general. "First," he tells his students, "you must *engage*. Form a relationship. Let people know you're there for the long haul." Second, *assess*. "In my thirty years as a social worker, I've never had someone come in and say, 'My life is going great.' I look for the hurt places but also for the resilient places. We build on strengths." Third, *generate alternatives/make a plan*. "Identify where you are now and where you would like to be and the steps that will bridge the chasm." Fourth, *implement*. Fifth, *evaluate*. "How do you know if the plan is working or not working?" Sixth, *bring things to a close*. Seventh, *follow up*. "Are the changes lasting over time?"

"In the real world," DeMattos says, "there's never a time when these elements are not in play. When you see this, you can't unsee it."

A CLOSING ROUND TABLE

At the conclusion of our second student round table, Chris Langworthy, who had poured much of her professional life into student field work, said that her faith in the future had been reaffirmed. The other veteran social workers tended to agree. To the extent that issues of healing, equality, and justice were much on the students' minds, the original notion for this book seemed to have become more nuanced. The global pandemic raged and a new and more liberal national administration was at work. In short, the social and political atmosphere was mixed. It was both encouraging and discouraging.

We resolved to do a last-minute, third round table, no longer face to face but by Zoom, to see if some sort of shift was detectable.

Debbie Shimizu—the social worker in our group most involved in state policy—recruited four bright young MSWs, all female. One was starting a doctorate. In her field work she had developed a sense of frustration resulting from her forays into advocacy. She was looking to have "the three little letters" after her name. She wanted not only to learn more but also to be taken more seriously regarding policy questions. She alone took up the question of the US presidency, saying Biden was an improvement but could be doing more.

Two of the students worked on gerontology projects. They likewise talked about their frustrations with government programs, seeing many holes and gaps in what needed to be done for the aged. Nonetheless they felt a level of gratification that comes from meaningful engagement. One was, at a young age, the team leader of a gerontology project. The other cut through the conversation by saying despite setbacks here and there she was essentially optimistic about making improvements to social services in the future. She announced that the glass is half full.

The fourth had resettled from Micronesia to study social work. She was acutely aware of the multi-layered problems facing Micronesian immigrants, most immediately their being disproportionately stricken by the coronavirus. At the time, she was dividing her work hours between a floor of Queen's Hospital serving the elderly and a floor coping with a second-wave overflow of virus infections. That she was composed and strong was in itself admirable, and her determination to help Micronesians in Hawai'i showed fight.

In brief, they were a mix of optimism and frustration. If the glass was half full, it was also half empty. Vaguely, several referred to the notion that social change can be developed from the bottom up and there is no point in getting mad and confronting authority figures. There was a basic sense of being up against daunting circumstances with no breakthroughs in sight—no New Deal, no War on Poverty.

At the end of the conversation, I took a quick survey. Who had heard of Clorinda Lucas? No one. I named the other seven figures whose stories are detailed in this book. The one name they recognized was Myron Thompson, being students of the Thompson School. I wrote an e-mail to my gang of four senior social workers: "I think they are really bright and caring, but with little sense of context to bolster bigger, more long-term thinking."

Debbie Shimizu was particularly taken aback because they had not heard of AQ McElrath, who so recently had been well-known and also was Debbie's personal hero. In a similar vein Susan Chandler wrote, "I find this quite depressing. It's the responsibility of the schools to teach students about the larger community and put the field of social work into perspective based on those who came before, not only in Hawai'i but in the history of social justice in America." Sharon Otagaki was disappointed but not surprised: "The work continues but I'm not aware of social workers who are leading big changes in our state. Leadership takes time and mentoring to develop, as well as networks with fellow social workers to promote big changes." Chris Langworthy weighed in with, "I feel more strongly than ever that social workers need mentors and icons. The field is much too difficult to go it alone."

All in all, we were spurred to push on to publication. If the social work of the 1960s and 1970s in Hawai'i has shown us something especially remarkable, it is that social work skills can translate well into activism and policy making at a high level. Be it affirmed: Social work equips people to work effectively across an almost unimaginably broad front of issues and problems. These we have in abundance.

I thought of the young woman who was twice orphaned and who nonetheless found herself constantly helping others, and who was commuting to UH while working full-time and completing her master's degree. She was eager to go out into the field and get to work. "The future of social work is like a bright star," she told us. "I see it in the passion and the ideas of my colleagues and my co-workers and in their capacity to keep pushing forward."

At our final meeting on editorial content, we addressed the question of a conclusion. Given the uncertainties of this crisis-laden time, we collectively took a deep breath. We had been refreshed by the reminders that social work consistently attracts people who want to make the world better. While most employment in the field of social work is about helping people cope, adapt, or grow modestly, the creative passion seeks breakthroughs. The work of social justice—of detecting, tracking, compiling, spotlighting, formulating, and advocating—emerges from encounters with suffering, inequity, and injustice.

Stepping back, as you do at an end point, it feels as if we—all of us as a community—are floating in an ill-defined mid-range. We hear a drum beating that sends a message of urgency. There is a reckoning coming that has to do with our unique three-way intersection: The moral and social future of the United States, the energy level and direction of the state of Hawai'i, and the regenerative and connecting power of the Hawaiian world. Social justice might be enhanced. It might be dashed. It might thrive or wither. The challenges are immense, but so are the possibilities. ✦

Index

About the Author

Tom Coffman has written widely about Hawai'i's social, political, and historical landscape. His books include *Catch A Wave*, *Nation Within*, *The Island Edge of America*, *Tadaima!* and, most recently, *Inclusion*, which was chosen to represent Hawai'i in the 2022 National Book Festival.

His work has received the Hawai'i Award for Excellence in Literature and three Best Non-Fiction of the Year awards from the Hawai'i Book Publishers Association. He has also received numerous awards for his documentary film-making.